The Trouble with ALCOHOL

America's Most Abused Drug

Tom Shipp

Fleming H. Revell Company
Old Tappan, New Jersey

Scripture quotations not otherwise identified are from the Revised Standard Version of the Bible, copyrighted 1946, 1952, © 1971 and 1973.

Scripture quotations identified NEB are from The New English Bible. © The Delegates of the Oxford University Press and the Syndics of the Cambridge University Press, 1961 and 1970. Reprinted by permission.

Scripture quotations identified KJV are from the King James Version of the Bible.

The Twelve Steps are from *Twelve Steps and Twelve Traditions*, copyright © 1952, by Alcoholics Anonymous World Services, Inc. Printed by permission of Alcoholics Anonymous World Services, Inc.

Library of Congress Cataloging in Publication Data

Shipp, Thomas J
    The trouble with alcohol.

    1. Alcoholism. 2. Alcoholics—Rehabilitation.
I. Title.
HV5035.S54   362.2'92   77-20148
ISBN 0-8007-0909-8

Contents

The Lovers Lane United Methodist Story

As the man who owned the wrecking yard led me through the jumble of rusting cars, I reflected that Bob couldn't have chosen a more symbolic place in which to hole up. Here were the dregs of what had once been sleek new cars, the pride of their owners. Now their fenders were crumpled, their glass shattered, their upholstery in tatters. And Bob looked just as cast-off as the old cars.

We found him lying on the backseat of a battered Ford. His face showed almost green through a two-week-old stubble of beard. His suit was rumpled and filthy. At his feet were a dozen empty bottles. The stench was unbearable. I had never seen such a sick man in my life.

"I let him sleep out here because it was raining. He didn't seem to have anywhere else to go," said the wrecking-yard owner. "I could see he needed help."

As he said these words I was aware he was looking me over, mentally shaking his head and wondering why on earth the church had sent such a young, inexperienced minister.

I was wondering the same thing myself. Here I was, in my first year at Perkins School of Theology at Southern Methodist University in Dallas. It was 1941. I had just begun work at Highland Park Methodist Church, supposedly as a student minister, not a counselor of alcoholics.

I'd never dealt with a drunk. I'd never been intoxicated myself. In fact I had never even tasted anything alcoholic in my life. I guess the closest I ever came to experiencing intoxication was the time I drank some cider that had been sitting on the back of my tractor for a whole day.

And now, suddenly, this alcoholic was my responsibility. He was a man who once had been a respected school principal in Texas. But when he was in his mid-thirties, he'd been persuaded to take a drink at a board-of-education meeting. After that it was all downhill for Bob. He drank so much that he finally deserted his family and disappeared from friends and relatives for a full year. Meanwhile his wife had divorced him. What was I going to do to bring healing to a man like that?

"I guess we'd better get him into my car," I said. We pulled him out of the old wreck. We threw his limp arms over our shoulders and half-dragged him to my auto.

"Whass going on?" the man mumbled as we laid him on my backseat.

"Don't worry, just lie still," I said. "We're going to get help for you."

And I really believed, as I drove back to the church, that someone would be able to cure him. Wouldn't the other ministers know what to do? After all, the only reason that the church secretary had handed me the phone when Bob's brother called by long distance was that no other minister was around. And it hadn't seemed to matter to Bob's brother that I was lowest on the staff. He seemed desperate to believe that the church would be able to help.

"This is the first we've heard from Bob since he left his wife," Bob's brother had said. "Could you find him and stay with him until I get there?"

"Of course," I said. "Where is he?"

"I don't know," Bob's brother said. "He was so drunk that all he could tell me was that he was in a wrecking yard on the highway. He didn't know the address or the name of the yard."

As I helped Bob stumble up the stairs to my office, I congratulated myself that I'd been able to find Bob with such skimpy directions. But once we were inside I had other things to think about. Bob was so sick he couldn't sit up in a chair. I suggested he lie on the floor and was relieved to see that he dropped off to sleep almost immediately.

After I phoned Bob's brother to tell him I had Bob safe with me, I began making calls to the other ministers.

"I'm sorry. I just don't know much about handling alcoholics," they told me. "Just do what you can until his brother arrives."

I called two doctors I knew in Highland Park's congregation.

"There's really very little you can do to help someone who drinks like that," both said. "I wish I knew a cure, but I don't."

Finally I called another doctor and asked him to enter Bob into a hospital.

"I can't do that," he said. "Hospitals don't accept people just because they're drunk."

As the hands on my watch crawled forward and Bob kept on sleeping, I began to realize the helplessness that alcoholics and their families then faced. Neither ministers nor doctors had any better ideas about how to rehabilitate an alcoholic than did I, a first-year theology student.

But didn't Bob need help? And hadn't I promised his brother I would stay with him? There seemed to be nothing to do but to take Bob home with me until his brother arrived.

At the tiny apartment in which my wife and I then lived, I put Bob in the only bed.

"It won't be long until his brother comes for him," I promised my wife. Then I got another phone call. Bob's brother had become suddenly ill. He was now in the hospital for emergency surgery. He would not be coming to Dallas after all. Could I please take care of Bob?

My wife moved into the little sitting area to sleep on the couch while I stayed with Bob. It was then that I began to realize fully just how terrible alcoholism truly is. By the second night Bob had begun to see little men crawling all around the room. I had to sit and hold his hand.

"Turn on more lights, more lights," he kept screaming.

We managed to struggle through three hectic days. Finally Bob was sober. I was pleased. In those days I was naive enough to believe that to cure alcoholism all you had to do was to dry a drunk out once and for all. While Bob had no home, didn't know where his wife was, and had no income, I could fix that. I found him a job at a Dallas bookstore and arranged for a place for him to stay.

I thought all would be well with Bob. Then he received his first paycheck and went off on another binge. When I tried to find him, neither his boss nor his landlord knew where he was. I thought perhaps he would call me, but he didn't. I began to see that I hadn't really helped Bob at all.

Then one afternoon when I was in the church office, a lady came by to pick up several copies of *The Upper Room*. This devotional booklet has a passage of Scripture, a "Thought for the Day," and a prayer for each day of the week.

"Do you mind telling me how you are using these?" I asked, not realizing just how important her answer would be for the alcoholics I wanted to help.

"I am an alcoholic," she said. "When I lived in Houston, I helped organize an Alcoholics Anonymous group. Since there is no AA in Dallas, I've been meeting with two others who have drinking problems. We use *The Upper Room* as a guide," she said.

I could see that Bob could get the help he needed in that kind of group. I told her about Bob's failure to stay sober and urged her to organize a real AA in Dallas. She and her friends began to work on it.

And then one day I got a call from the wrecking-yard owner, telling me that "my drunk" was back. I could hardly wait to see what had happened to Bob.

Much to my dismay, I found Bob looking every bit as drunk and sick as he had been the first time I saw him. But he seemed glad to see me. As I took him home with me this time, I knew who could help him. I called the lady who had had experience with AA. She and a man who was also a recovering alcoholic came right out.

Together we got Bob sober, found him another job at another bookstore, and arranged another place for him to stay. Later, as the AA group became organized, Bob was one of the first to join.

Bob had three struggling years before he really got on his feet. But from that day until his death, he did not have another drink. I cannot begin to tell you the good that he did or the number of people that he helped.

It didn't take long for the word to get around. Even though I was still only a seminary student and youth pastor, I soon began to receive calls from families and alcoholics who were desperate for help. Even though I had no training, no experience, no authorities to consult other than my friends in AA, I spent many of my days while in seminary aiding people in trouble with alcohol.

During the first three to four years, I helped alcoholics on a one-to-one basis, doing what I could to get these people into AA if at all possible. My reputation followed me right into my first appointment after being graduated from seminary, when I was offered the opportunity to start Lovers Lane United Methodist Church in 1945.

On a sunny October Sunday morning I preached my first sermon as the pastor of that church in the small two-bedroom rented home in which the first few members were meeting. There were seventeen people in Sunday school and twenty-two at church services, including my wife, my brother, and his wife. At the end of the service that morning, four alcoholics joined.

The days that followed were doubly exciting. Not only were we building a new congregation, but we were also helping a group of people rejected by society and forgotten by the church.

As of yet the AA group as we know it today was not really established. Furthermore there was a real stigma attached to joining. I kept getting more and more calls for assistance, even though my only qualifications were that I loved and cared for alcoholics and saw them just as people with a problem.

At this time I still hadn't learned the difficult lesson that one person cannot get other persons sober and keep them that way. I didn't understand that all you can do is give aid and perhaps create in others the desire to stay sober.

I didn't fully realize the role of the church, either. How embarrassing it must have been to our neighbors, and church members too, when scarcely a day passed that there wasn't a drunk in my home or in our church! But I thought I could sober up the whole community single-handedly.

Then something happened that discouraged me a great deal at the same time that it delivered a message. One after another, all of these sobered-up friends began to slip back into drinking again. They just couldn't stay sober. And who did they blame? They laid it on me, the church, even God!

The day I finally realized that I myself needed help seems amusing to me now, despite the real tragedy surrounding those events.

Early one morning I received a call from a man I'll call

Mr. Smith, asking me to help his wife.

"She's drinking again," he said. So I promised to come quickly. Evidently Mrs. Smith had heard the conversation; because when I rang the Smiths' doorbell, she burst through the door and sailed right past me, wearing nothing but a nightgown.

"Catch her!" yelled Mr. Smith, who came running after her.

Without thinking, I took up the chase when suddenly it hit me. *This is certainly a nice picture,* I told myself. *A preacher chasing a woman in her nightgown! What would I do if I caught her, anyway?*

So I yelled at the husband, "You catch her. I'll head her off if she comes down the alley!"

It just seemed I was "on call" all that day, working with one alcoholic after another. At 11:30 that night I found myself going back to visit the Smiths' again, this time with a recovered alcoholic. We didn't get away until 2:30 A.M. At that late hour it seemed easier for me to let my helper take my car and drive himself home than for me to do it. But I had no sooner gotten to bed than I received a call from the Smiths' neighbor. It seemed that she had a drinking problem too, and she wanted me to help her get sober. I told her that since I had no car there was no way for me to get to her house.

About thirty minutes later my doorbell rang and I found a taxi driver who insisted that I was his fare. Mrs. Smith's neighbor had sent a cab for me. My wife and I got dressed and went to see her that night.

"This is the smartest thing you've ever done," I told Mrs. Smith's neighbor. "You've asked for help." Then, all at once, tired as I was, I realized that this woman had really acted much more intelligently than I had. Because she knew to ask for assistance whereas I had been trying to get the whole community sober all by myself. It dawned on me right there that I too needed others to help me.

But whom could I ask? There was no money for hiring staff and in fact no one trained in the field of alcoholism even if I could pay them. So I turned to the alcoholics themselves. I thought that the way to help them and also help myself was to organize a group of alcoholics who would meet with me at the church twice a week.

This plan seemed good but was destined for failure for two reasons. First of all, the people who met with me were quickly identified by church members as "the drunk group." They could not be accepted as simply members of Lovers Lane as everyone else was. I learned this drawback when I suggested the name of a recovered alcoholic to the committee selecting nominees for our new church administrative board. His name was immediately rejected.

"We don't want a drunk for one of our officers," committee members said.

Secondly I found that recovering alcoholics within the group itself sometimes inadvertently felt rejection by the pastor and other members. Those who had not yet recovered very well were not called on to help those having serious problems. They felt unwanted.

Our group didn't meet at the church very long. But some good did come of it. For now I knew many people on whom I could call at any hour of the day or night to be a friend to alcoholics who needed a visit. And an amazing thing happened. As I called on these recovering alcoholics to assist problem drinkers, they stayed sober themselves. They became healthier in their feelings about themselves and their attitudes toward me, the church, and God.

I learned that when alcoholics are placed on the giving side of recovery as well as the receiving side, they help themselves. After all, what higher compliment could be paid to alcoholics than for their minister to ask for their assistance? I, in turn, had no need to ask a committee for permission to invite them to serve, either.

For this reason, when a group which wanted to split off from the downtown AA and form a neighborhood AA asked if they could meet at my church, I knew what my decision had to be.

"I don't think you ought to meet at the church, because that's the way you get identified as just a bunch of drunks," I told them. "But I think the church should help you find a better place to meet."

This we did. And since that time, no other Dallas AA groups have attempted to meet in churches.

I really felt it was to AA's advantage to have a location that belonged entirely to them. They could meet there during the day if they wanted, or they could bring people there who needed help and stay with them. There were no other places in Dallas at that time to meet that need.

In my mind I saw AA as a place of fellowship, a program that would help a person gain sobriety. I saw it as a group of people banded together to strengthen and help each other.

I identified the church as an extended arm of AA. It was the place where alcoholics could find their way back into the life of the community. In the church they could find help for their problems without being identified by their problem.

Many members of AA with whom I had been working did unite with the church and become active. The proof that we were on the right track came one night at another nominating-committee meeting. On his own, one member nominated an alcoholic to be chairman of our new administrative board. The nomination carried unanimously. In the community of the church, this alcoholic was thought of as a member of Lovers Lane who had a place to serve. He did a beautiful job!

As the years have passed, alcoholics have provided great leadership for Lovers Lane United Methodist—as teachers, committee members, workers of all types. Their service has helped them not only find their faith in God and plug into the Higher Power but also to regain confidence in themselves, in others, and in the world in which they live.

From the very beginning, however, I did not feel that I should be working with alcoholics for the purpose of getting them to join my church. In some cases I felt this result would be one of the most unchristian actions possible.

When John asked to join my church, I quickly realized that his thinking was immature and selfish. I had to really work with him to keep him from doing it.

"Why do you want to join Lovers Lane, when your family has been active in your own church for fifteen years?" I asked, fully realizing that, like many alcoholics, John had not set foot in his church in years. He was too embarrassed to go.

"Your church does a lot for alcoholics. You understand us," John said. "That's why I want to join."

"Let's think about it in another way," I said. "You've belonged to that other church for years. Your family belongs there and attends faithfully. Who ministered to them during the last ten to fifteen years while you've been having this problem?"

"I guess my church has," John said.

"Didn't you tell me that it was your minister who gave your wife the kind of strength and courage she needed just to hold on all these years?" I asked, while John nodded sheepishly. "Have you thought about what it would mean to the family that has stood by you and loves you to make them leave their church? I know that you love them. Have you ever thought about what it would mean to them if you would say, 'I want to go to Sunday school and church with you'?" But John just frowned.

"There's no one there who understands about alcoholics. They don't have anything to offer us. I don't think they care about us," he said.

I didn't argue the point. "But look, John," I said. "I'm not going to run off. You can still come to church here. We have three services every Sunday morning. If you come to our early service, you will still have time to go home and take your family to your church."

Actually I already knew a member of AA who belonged to John's church. I suggested we might meet and have lunch together. We did. And when they realized they both belonged to the same church and had the same problems, John had a whole new feeling toward that person and that church.

The next Sunday he was at our 8:00 A.M. service. Then he went home and took his family to Sunday school and church. Since then he has thanked me for not letting him join Lovers Lane.

"You'll never know what going to church together did for my family," he said later. "It united us, deepened our trust level with one another. We were put together as a family again, and that restored their self-respect in the community. I can't begin to tell you how that church has ministered to me and my family."

I'm convinced that in any strong rehabilitation program, alcoholics have to find their Saviour and Lord. They need that Higher Power that can give them a sense of well-being and worth, of being somebody who is loved. In addition they need a community of people, even beyond the group therapy or AA, to which they can have a sense of belonging.

Today I receive calls week after week from professionals, other pastors, and seminary students. They all want to see the organization that helps alcoholics at Lovers Lane. I just have to say to them, "It's here. It's the Lord. It's God. It's this community. It's the church. It's the staff that has a sense of caring."

Yes, the church must do its job. But if AA can do something better than we can, why should we duplicate? What the church must do is support AA and other such groups in all they're attempting to do.

The church can also support community growth in the fight against alcoholism. A judge once called me and asked me to get some information out to the public.

"We need to let people know that alcoholics can be helped," he said. It was then that we invited Marty Mann to come to Dallas and speak. It was perhaps the first large gathering of this kind to attend a public meeting. Then a group of us began raising money and support for the establishment of the Dallas Council on Alcoholism.

The same thing happened at the state level when a group I was meeting with said, "Something needs to be done about alcoholism within the state." A group of us met with the governor and other interested citizens, raised the money, and helped set up the first Texas Commission on Alcoholism, which has since served this state ably.

We have also worked one by one with the professionals who so desperately need the church's help—the doctors, psychiatrists, and psychologists.

Since a small percentage of alcoholics need hospitalization, we have worked to establish clinics. Some were not so good. Some went by the wayside, but others have served a real purpose and a great need in the community.

We've talked to hospital administrators, helping them see that often they have treated alcoholics who entered under the guise of having some other physical ailment. So now hospital doors have opened to alcoholics being treated for alcoholism. All kinds of programs have been established.

Lovers Lane United Methodist has not set up an organization within the church but has helped establish a wider framework within the community and state. Ministers and churches who have the right approach can be a key to all the other programs that are giving alcoholics assistance within the community. The church's paramount mission, of course, is leading alcoholics and their families to a living faith and offering a fellowship beyond that of the secular groups.

It has not always been easy to keep the doors of Lovers Lane open to those who need help or to those suffering people who need to realize that there actually is a way back to a healthy life.

One day my bishop called me and said, "There are people in your church who are unhappy. You're spending too much time with alcoholics." I realized he was right. I had to minister to more than just a special group of people who were in trouble with alcohol.

And I recall another committee that went to the bishop and asked him to "do something."

"We do not like our minister's going into taverns and taking drunks home with him. This kind of conduct is going to hurt our church and our minister too," they said.

I had to explain to the bishop that Lovers Lane could not reach out to people who needed help unless we answered needs wherever they happened—whether it was in the roughest tavern, on the murkiest block of Skid Row, or inside the most fashionable house in the city.

"If the church does not extend a helping hand with a sense of caring, love, and concern, then it has failed to fulfill its ministry," I said.

To me the alcoholic is no different from any other human being who is sick. Did not Jesus prophesy that He will say on Judgment Day:

". . . Come, O blessed of my Father, inherit the kingdom . . . for I was hungry and you gave me food, I was thirsty and you gave me drink, I was a stranger and you welcomed me, I was naked and you clothed me, I was sick and you visited me, I was in prison and you came to me." Then the righteous will answer him, "Lord, when did we see thee hungry and feed thee, or thirsty and give thee drink? And when did we see thee a stranger and welcome thee, or naked and clothe thee? And when did we see thee sick or in prison and visit thee?" And the King will answer them, "Truly I say to you, as you did it to one of the least of these my brethren, you did it to me."

Matthew 25:34–40

I told my bishop, "I will do all in my power to help my people understand this Scripture, both by example and word."

Surely Lovers Lane has become a congregation that loves and cares about people, wherever they are and in whatever condition they may be. Our growth has never suffered. Today we have eight thousand members, among them five hundred recovered alcoholics. We have also helped countless others who have returned to their own churches to become active and involved.

No one can draw a chart that shows all the organizations and groups with which Lovers Lane United Methodist has worked. But it is our hope that the lives of the people who have been touched will prove that the way pointed to by Jesus is the way to help alcoholics too.

Despite the many community organizations working with alcoholism, not a week passes that we don't get at least ten calls from new individuals who are trying to find help either for themselves or someone they love who is in trouble with alcohol. At Lovers Lane the finger is not pointed, or judgment given. Instead we try to point to a way that will lead to life, a new life, in Jesus Christ.

2

The Great Deceiver

Jim was in trouble with alcohol, and he didn't know why.

"At first I thought alcohol was helping me," he told me the first time he came to see me. At thirty Jim was still a young man, slim and almost boyish looking; but his face was puffy. Dark circles rimmed his eyes. As he talked he gripped the chair with a shaking hand.

"I started using alcohol because I was having insomnia. I just didn't seem to be able to turn off my mind at night. But after only a few sips of bourbon, my heart would stop pounding and my thoughts stopped whirling. Before you knew it, I was out. The next day I woke up rested and ready.

"And then one day I had an important meeting with my banker. I took a little drink beforehand to calm my nerves. I felt more relaxed, and the meeting went well.

"But then a strange thing happened. It took more and more drinks for me to be able to sleep at night. And there seemed to be so many times that I needed to unwind at the office that I finally started keeping a bottle in my desk drawer, where it was handy. I drank more and more, but my tensions got worse and worse.

"It got to where I didn't have any control over my drinking. Look at me, I'm only thirty, and I've lost my business because of my drinking, and I'm in danger of losing my wife and my children too.

21

"I thought that alcohol would hold me together. It did not. Alcohol deceived me," he said.

For many who find themselves unable to cope in a world grown more competitive, alcohol seems the likeliest escape. To blot out the disillusionment of a life that is strangely empty, many turn to the bottle. Young people drink to avoid the knowledge that they have no goals in life. Sometimes whole families imbibe to soothe the hurts caused by the stresses between parents and children.

But alcohol does not alleviate pain. It does not undo physical discomfort or make today's frenzied rat race into the good old days of yesterday. Alcohol is a great deceiver. If used over a long period of time, it increases rather than decreases every kind of problem.

The person who observed Jim's and Kay's lives from the outside would find it hard to understand why Jim had developed a problem. Jim had been a football hero in college. His lovely wife had been popular too. Now they had two fine children and a large home. From outward appearances their lives seemed as perfect as that of any of the "beautiful people" who star in television shows.

But their lives also point up one startling fact about life in twentieth-century America. Despite the freedom from physical discomfort, many people now suffer more than ever before from mental distress.

Jim has painful memories of growing up in a small town as the eldest of eight children. The clothes he wore were always the shabbiest in his class, no matter how hard he worked at paper routes and lawn mowing to make extra money.

"More than anything in the world," he told me, "I wanted to have a home, clothes, a car that were not just as good as our neighbor's. I wanted them better than anyone else's in town."

With this determination Jim excelled in everything from school studies and sports to work. He earned an athletic scholarship to one of the finest universities in the United States.

But while he always played first string, he never made All-American. While his grade-point average was above 3.0, he never made Phi Beta Kappa. He joined a fraternity and was popular with both sexes, but he was never elected president of the fraternity. Somehow he just never could be "good enough" at anything he wanted to do.

Then Jim fell in love with a coed who was one of the most popular girls on the campus. Kay loved him too. She had never known what it meant to be without a big monthly allowance for clothes and entertainment, but she told Jim she could do without all that. They were married during Jim's senior year.

Unconsciously Jim felt that he was just not quite good enough for Kay, but his parents felt just the opposite. "You know how to work," they often said, "but Kay knows only how to play."

Once out of the university, Jim landed what was considered an excellent job for a new graduate. But compared to his father-in-law's position, it was nothing. Kay could not believe how small her clothing budget was. Soon her parents were buying all her clothes. When the two children arrived, they picked up the bill for everything from booties to winter coats.

Now Jim felt he had to make a better living for Kay. He borrowed some money and went into business with an old football buddy. He worked longer hours and was rarely at home. Even so, the business was not producing as much income as he hoped. That was when the insomnia and the drinking began.

His drinking got so bad that Kay couldn't seem to stand the sight of him anymore. He drank more. The tensions got worse. He lost the business and was on the verge of losing Kay and the children too when he decided to come to me for help.

Like most people who use alcohol to change their mental attitudes, Jim did not realize that it is a great deceiver. Among all drugs, it could well be the most dangerous—because it is the most deceptive.

Alcohol appears to be helping to solve a problem at the very same time that it is aggravating it. Alcohol never gets in a hurry. It always works by degrees. It never pushes, lest it become obvious what it is doing.

Like a termite undermining the foundations of a beautiful home, alcohol never lets its destruction be seen. It always hides its tracks—until at last the whole house caves in.

For instance, people who are addicted to other drugs soon become tolerant toward their effect. Their bodies require more and more of the drug to get the same amount of release. Not alcohol—some people who are in trouble with booze may find that they need less and less to get the same effect. Alcohol deceives them into thinking all is well because they are drinking less.

For every use of alcohol, there is a deception. Let's look at what alcohol promises, and what it delivers instead.

Alcohol says, "If you are nervous, use me and I will quiet you down. I will calm your stormy waters." But I have never known an alcoholic who was not nervous and jumpy. While alcohol is calming the drinker, it is also creating a new dimension in nervousness.

"Use me, and I will give you rest and sleep," says alcohol. But for alcoholics drinking permits only an artificial kind of slumber that brings no rest. Their sleep lasts only for short periods of time. Almost always alcoholics wake against their wishes early in the morning and are not able to go back to sleep. Alcohol does not bring rest. It robs alcoholics of sleep.

For the gourmand, alcohol promises "bon appetit." Yet most alcoholics find it very difficult to stomach food, and all are malnourished. The reason is that alcohol does not have to be digested. Instead it passes through the upper intestines, directly into the bloodstream. Alcohol contains no satisfying food values; yet it will be absorbed by the body before real nourishment. Even if a drinker eats a balanced diet, alcohol prevents the good nutrients from entering the bloodstream. Instead these nutrients convert into waste products to be stored up as fat while the body still cries out for energy. People who do not have the ability to store up fat will in fact lose weight while drinking.

Thus, a person may drink and eat but still end up with malnutrition even though his body is fat. Alcohol may give drinkers an appetite, but if they become dependent on it, they will often starve.

For others alcohol's promise is to make them brave and courageous. But most alcoholics are not self-confident. They are afraid. The very first alcoholic I helped was so afraid that I had to put a two-hundred-watt light bulb in the lamp beside the bed. I had to sit beside him and hold his hand.

"I don't know why I am afraid," he said to me. "Up until recently, alcohol removed my fear. Now it seems to make it worse. When I drink, I become afraid of everything. I'm afraid to go to sleep, afraid to wake up, afraid to see people, afraid to be left alone, afraid to get up—afraid, afraid, afraid!" Then grabbing me, he screamed, "O God, I am scared. Please don't leave me!"

A young lady once said to me, "When I first started drinking, I could go out on a dance floor. There wasn't any step I couldn't do. I wasn't afraid to dance with the best of partners.

"But I finally found that after a period of time alcohol was very jealous, refusing to let me have another partner. Alcohol made me step only to its own music. Finally I became so afraid that I would not even go near a dance floor—even if I had plenty of alcohol beforehand."

And I recall what a young man who had a drinking problem said to me: "I wanted to make love to my wife, but I couldn't. The first time this happened, I blamed her. I told her it was all her fault. It had nothing to do with me. But then it happened over and over again. I went to one doctor and then another. Finally I came to you. You suggested it might be helpful for me to try to stop drinking while we worked on the marriage problem. It was during that period of sobriety that I began to see what had happened to me.

"Alcohol had taken away my manhood. It had begun to make all kinds of excuses for what had taken place in my life. I was being robbed," he said.

How subtle, how shrewd, how keen is the approach of the Great Deceiver. If you yourself are in trouble with alcohol, you should listen to those persons who are close to you and love you. They may be the only ones who care enough to let you know how you are being deceived—by a very sly wolf dressed up in grandmother's clothing, who tells you how wonderful you are at the same time he is getting ready to grab you.

Today alcohol is destroying the physical, emotional, and spiritual well-being of uncounted men, women, young people, and even children. It threatens all cultures, every social level, people of all religious backgrounds.

It is impossible to pinpoint all the complex factors that have made a slavish dependence on alcohol one of the most pressing problems in America today. But certainly there are a number of apparent causes of which we should all be aware.

Despite today's shorter workweeks, push-button entertainment, and general affluence, millions of people find themselves simply bored. Today holds no interest, tomorrow no future. Misery and monotony lie in wait day after day, week after week, month after month.

But alcohol promises a way of forgetting the emptiness of

life. In fact we are led to believe that by drinking we will fill all our days with fun and fascination. Booze will meet all our needs.

Everyone from teenagers to the oldest grandparents may be afflicted with the empty-life feeling. This monotony is no respecter of the rich or the poor, the employed or the unemployed, the singles or the married.

Young people especially seem to be restless and uneasy about finding their identities today. They do not seem to sense a destiny as have past generations. For the first time in the history of the human race, people are not a product of their goals, for they make no goals. To help them feel better about themselves, they turn to alcohol.

Some young people, of course, simply find it impossible to stand up to the pressures of peer groups who are drinking. They believe that alcohol will bring them friendships. Once they are deceived by alcohol and their friends, they seem to develop a complete lack of concern for themselves and those who love them.

"No one has a right to tell me what I can or cannot do," they often say. "It is my life to do with as I please." Only too late do they realize what they have done to it.

Even the family, which used to be the fundamental nurturing unit in our society, today becomes the initiator of alcohol dependency for both parents and children. Now many fathers work away from the home for weeks at a time or are separated from their children by divorce. With the role of both father and mother changing radically, much tension is created within the family. Single parents struggle with their double responsibilities for the livelihood as well as the training of the children.

Alcohol promises to overcome these stresses and make the home a pleasant place for all the family. But in reality alcohol simply causes parents to train their children to become alcoholics.

But perhaps the main reason why people today are being jet-propelled into alcoholism is their illusion that the ideal life is one of ease, devoid of trouble. It is entirely natural to want to avoid suffering. The search for ways to escape discomfort has led the human race to invent everything from electrical power mowers and dishwashers to central heating and air-conditioning.

In today's world the ultimate goal seems to be to eliminate even the slightest degree of discomfort, whether it be physical or mental.

Religion has contributed to this point of view. Who has not heard the plea, "Come to Jesus Christ and leave your burden and pain"? But a study of the life of Jesus shows that it certainly was not without pain.

Hear His prayer at Gethsemane: "My Father, if it be possible, let this cup pass from me" (Matthew 26:39). His cry on the cross was: "My God, my God, why hast thou forsaken me?" (Matthew 27:46).

He certainly died one of the most agonizing of all deaths—on a cross—at a premature age. His faith did not give Him a life of ease. But it did give Him strength to deal with pain, weariness, and disease—and still live life to the fullest. It gave Him the ability to fulfill His purpose in life.

"Use me, and I will give you a life of ease and comfort. I will help you forget, block out all your pain, make you feel tall. I will solve every one of your problems," says the Great Deceiver.

Do not be misled. The problems which alcohol promises to cure will only worsen for people who become the victims of alcohol. When that happens only a good guide and a plainly marked road map can lead back to a healthy life.

3

Which Highway Shall I Take?

As I opened the door to my waiting room one afternoon, I saw a young man who was obviously nervous and just as plainly in need of help. Standing in front of my secretary's desk, he kept shifting from foot to foot. His eyes flitted from my secretary's face to the church member waiting for his scheduled appointment with me, then darted quickly to the pictures on the walls. Finally they rested on me.

"Couldn't I just see you right now for a few minutes?" he asked, running a hand through his shaggy mass of uncombed hair.

I could see he had come to my office on impulse, and now he was fearful and doubtful as to whether he ought to have come. If I suggested he make an appointment and come back, it would be too painful. He probably would never come again. I turned to the church member, one of my committee chairmen and a person I knew to be understanding.

"Would you mind if I visited with Jim just for a moment?" I asked. I was pleased when he told me to go ahead.

In my office I scarcely had time to offer the young man a comfortable chair before he came right to the point. He was in trouble with alcohol.

"I feel as if I'm on an expressway with all the other cars pushing and crowding. I can no longer read the signs, and I'm lost. I can't find an exit, and I'm afraid I'm going to have a terrible wreck." He put his face in his hands, almost sobbing.

"The worst part of all is that even if I do get off this expressway, I'm not sure I can find the road back. O God, I hurt! Isn't there a way out of all this mess?"

"Of course there is, Jim," I said. "But it's not a superhighway. The road to getting off alcohol is one of reconstruction and rebuilding. The highway is not well marked. The road map is difficult to read. There are detours that can be misleading and even hazardous. Sometimes you have to retrace your steps in order to go ahead. Sometimes you have motor trouble. But there's one thing about it. It's not a dead end."

Jim shook his head. "It sounds impossible," he said.

"But it's not a road you have to travel alone," I said. "Invite someone to travel with you, someone who has knowledge of the same road you will be traveling."

"Who would want to do that?" said Jim.

"There are many who by reason of devotion or a sense of caring and love will count it an honor and a privilege to be a fellow traveler with you on the road toward sobriety, health, and peace," I said. "Jim, please don't try to travel it alone, for the trip will be lonely, empty, long, and far more difficult if you do."

"Can you find someone who will tell me what to do?" Jim asked.

"No, I can't," I said. "I can help you find someone to go on the journey with you, but first there are some things that you must do."

"What's that?" Jim asked.

"First you have to make a decision—a big one," I said. "It's a critical decision, because it will affect you and the people around you and their future too. The decision you make will determine which road you're going to travel."

"What kind of a decision do you mean?" Jim asked. "I've never been very good at decision making."

Like so many of the other people I had seen who were in

trouble with alcohol, Jim was avoiding making the tough decision himself. He had never thought he had to worry about alcohol, because he felt that when the time came to stop drinking, he would just automatically know what to do. But that was far from the truth. Now I could see he was in hopes that I would make the decision for him.

"I just usually make decisions by instinct, intuition, or spur-of-the-moment impulses," Jim was saying. "Or I do whatever is easiest or what I like to do. Come to think of it, someone else usually decides for me."

The truth was that Jim was an expert at avoiding making decisions! He felt all he had to do was to let "life" decide for him. What he did not realize was that every time we fail to make a decision or a choice, we are, in fact, making one anyway. When we leave it up to "life" to decide, we allow someone or something else to make the decision. In Jim's case he was really allowing alcohol itself to make the decision to go on drinking. The sad part about it is that regardless of who or what makes the choice, we have to live with it and pay the price.

Decision making is the process of selecting the best road out of all possible roads. Perhaps you too are in trouble with alcohol, and you are no longer content to merely accept what someone or something thinks is good for you.

If you do want to decide for yourself what is the best course of action out of all possible alternatives, then it is vital to become fully conscious of those decision-making skills you already have and of the ones you need to learn.

First of all, what is most important for you in your life? What is your problem? What is the decision to be made? The choices must be based on your own criteria, not what your parents, your spouse, your children, or even the preacher, or your doctor think is important or is the problem. Only by making your own decisions will you be able to live by them.

But it is easier to talk about decision making than actually to make decisions. We have to separate what we really want from what we think we want. We must search for information about ourselves that speaks only to the problem and the decision.

Then we must look for all the possible alternatives. We must realize that the highway that is a good alternative for one person may be a road to failure for another.

As Jim sat in my office that afternoon, he was hurting. He was embarrassed at what he had done and eager to make a change in his life. He would have to make a decision as to whether he would continue to travel down the road of drinking or choose another path. But how would he feel tomorrow?

Right away I suggested that he answer a set of questions which I have found helpful to people who are in trouble with alcohol. Actually I have three sets of questions that I use, depending on whether drinkers are in the initial, the intermediate, or the final stages of alcoholism. All are aimed at helping drinkers identify problems and make decisions.

The first set of questions, for those who are wondering if they are in trouble with alcohol, is as follows:

1. Do I have an intense personal reason for drinking? In other words, is my reason for drinking something other than social?

2. Am I experiencing a meaningful change from the use of alcohol? Do I drink to relieve tension, fears, anxieties, or inhibitions?

3. Do I find myself involved increasingly in thought about alcohol? Am I thinking about the problem of supply when I should be thinking about other things?

4. Are most of my friends heavy drinkers?

5. Has my drinking become more secretive, more guarded?

6. Am I drinking more often and more heavily than in the past? Am I kidding myself that by drinking beer or wine I am cutting down? Do I tell myself I am handling my problem because I maintain periods of not drinking at all in between alcoholic bouts?

7. When I start drinking, do I end up drinking more than I intended to drink? Do I find drunkenness occurring at closer intervals?

8. Have I failed to remember what occurred during a drinking period last night, yesterday, or even a longer period ago?

9. Do I feel guilty, defensive, or angry when someone wants to talk to me about my drinking?

10. Am I sneaking my drinks?

11. Have I stopped sipping my drinks and instead find myself gulping or tossing them down quickly?

12. Do I lie about my drinking?

These are questions that help people decide whether they are or are not in trouble with alcohol. With the problem identified, they are ready to reach a decision.

Those who did not reach a decision at the initial period soon progress to a middle stage of alcoholism. In this intermediate phase, defensive thinking is apparent. Drinkers begin to lose control of the manner in which they drink as well as their behavior. They can no longer stop drinking when they choose.

Questions for drinkers who have reached the second stage of alcoholism are these:

1. Am I greatly concerned about protecting my supply? Have I developed an alibi system? Do I rationalize, or resent and suspect others? Do I find it necessary to lie to my employer, relatives, or friends to hide my drinking?

2. Have I lost control? Can I really stop drinking once I start? Do I find I need a drink to get over a drink? Do I want to drink alone? Have I become antisocial in my behavior?

3. Do I feel that other people are watching me?

4. Am I unduly critical of others such as my spouse, children, or the people with whom I work? Do I find a scapegoat rather than a solution to my problems? Is there always someone or something that I can blame for my drinking too much?

5. Has my behavior caused me to lose friends, family, and/or jobs?

6. Are people afraid of me while I am drinking?

7. Has another person—spouse, friend, fellow worker, or anyone else—said something to me about my drinking behavior?

At this intermediate stage, drinkers have not yet lost their health, their jobs, their families, their self-respect, or their self-confidence. They still have mental freedom and can make a decision. However, if they, like Jim, do not get off the highway to alcoholism at this intermediate stage, then they are in for real trouble. Beyond it they will find few exits. The road they will travel will be most painful.

I asked Jim the following questions, which are those which will help a person in the final stages of alcoholism to reach a decision:

1. Do I really have a choice as to whether or not I can drink? No matter what my determination to stop, do I seem completely powerless over alcohol?

2. Do I drink for days or weeks at a time?

3. When I try to get off alcohol, do I develop the "shakes"?

4. Have my fears become worse? Am I more hostile

toward others? Am I constantly afraid of something, but I do not know what?

5. Have I run out of excuses for what I am doing? Are there no more scapegoats around, no one to blame?

As I asked Jim those questions in my office that afternoon, I wished that he had asked himself the first set of questions while he was in the initial stage. I wished that his problem had been revealed to him early and that he had explored the alternatives available to him and had made a decision. If he had, he would not now be sitting in my office, his hair uncombed, his eyes betraying his misery.

I asked Jim what goals he wanted to set for himself.

"What I want most of all is to be a healthy person, a whole person," Jim said quietly. But in almost the same breath he said bitterly, "If only I could turn back the clock and just start my life over again!"

He did not see the endless, realistic possibilities open to him even at this stage of his life. Like many who find themselves in trouble with alcohol, Jim was afraid to try a new road, for he knew that he would fail to travel it. Hadn't he secretly promised himself time and time again that "things will change. It won't happen again"? And yet nothing had changed.

Besides, other well-meaning people had told him over and over again that there was only one road open for him to take. There were no alternatives, they said. Yet the road they chose just didn't work for Jim.

I hoped that Jim would set his goals that afternoon and let me help him explore the many roads he could travel to achieve them. But like so many other drinkers, Jim was unable to trust. He wanted to rely on his own sick thinking.

"There's no way out," Jim said. "Living without alcohol

is impossible and living with it is too painful. I bleed a little more each day.''

He knew that if he stopped drinking, he would experience all the horrors of hell that only the chemical of alcohol could relieve. If he continued to drink, it meant death.

Suicide was the only method Jim could see for dealing with his problem. He would not consider the alternatives, the roads so obvious to me, that could lead him out of his troubled life and into a better one.

Due to his dependence on alcohol, Jim had lost his mental freedom. Since he had reached the chronic stage of alcoholism, he was unable to make a decision or choose an alternative. Now his only hope was that someone would act for him. Hospital and medical care were imperative. He would have to allow himself to be taken care of by others and to receive treatment.

If Jim could be "dried out," an evaluation of his problem could be made. Alcohol could be removed from his system so that he would be in a condition to make a decision and choose an alternate road to life.

I am happy to report that Jim did recover and find the highway that led him to a new and healthy existence. But he would not have found it, nor would he have been able to travel it, had it not been for the many people and resources that came to his rescue.

Only a small percentage of people who are in trouble with alcohol have to be hospitalized. And most persons have not reached a stage in their drinking where decision making is impossible.

But people who are in trouble with alcohol must be able to clarify their own values in order to make an intelligent decision. They must even question the sources of their own value system, because these sources may be misleading. They may not be fruitful.

Are your sources dependable, reliable? Do they have

your best interest at heart? Against what background do you test your value system?

As a Christian I find there is no better test than to stand my value sources up before Jesus Christ. There are other sources too—such as the family, friends, peers, the church, or school.

When you have tested your value system, then use it in selecting the best alternative for you. People in trouble with alcohol must review their own behavior, their own actions. They must truthfully look at the road they are traveling and see where it leads. Beware of using road maps set up by friends. Choose instead what you will do and the direction you will travel, according to whether or not it suits *your* actual needs, not someone else's.

Ask yourself:

How am I spending my time?

Where am I spending it?

How have I spent my energy?

Do I spend my time drinking when I should be doing other things?

Have I spent time, money, and energy on alcohol when I didn't have it?

Critical decisions are not easy, And there are others who would like to make a decision for you, because they will not have to pay the consequences or take the risks. With any decision you make yourself there will be a risk involved. But you can't do anything in life without taking a risk. And you can reduce the risk by learning all the facts about it that you can.

Project all the possible consequences of the decisions to be made. Also, what are the consequences if you are unwilling to make a decision at all?

Look back and see what you have been betting your life on. Are the odds for you or against you? Do you have a chance of ending up a winner?

4

How to Get Help
From Those Around You

I was on the point of walking out the door of my office one Saturday morning, when the telephone rang. It was a lady asking when she might set up an appointment with me.

"Is it an emergency?" I asked. Her voice hesitated for a moment.

"No, but I've got a drinking problem, and I'd like to see you as soon as possible," she said. We set the appointment for the following week.

When Mary came in, I saw an attractive woman in her early forties, wearing expensive clothes. Her hair was perfectly arranged in the latest style. Her makeup was just right. But something was missing in the way Mary came across. Her cool and reserved manner made it appear that she almost felt she was doing me a favor by coming in. But then she lit a cigarette, and I could see her hand shaking. Suddenly this woman who had seemed so composed was asking me, "How do I get help from those around me?"

This is a question I so often hear! Mary, like so many others in trouble with alcohol, had turned away from people all the years she had been drinking. She had suffered defeat in her relations with both friends and family.

Even though she had been trying very hard to get sober for the past five years, she felt she had made little progress. No one wanted to help. Her husband and teenage children seemed to think she wasn't trying very hard, or surely they wouldn't come home and find her drunk. The friends she had had years before had long since given up inviting her places, because Mary always arrived in a stupor.

"Everyone's stopped trying because I've let them down so many times," Mary said. "But I really think I could get sober if there was someone who would be a friend to me. Can you tell me how I can get help?"

I had no reason to doubt that this woman was reaching out. She seemed driven to find a better way of life. Yet I could see that while Mary was asking for someone to help, she did not have any trust or faith in another person. Neither friends nor family could respond in a positive way unless Mary could demonstrate her belief that they could help.

Distrust closes the door to support that might come from those around you. People who have no faith in themselves will find it very difficult to trust any other person. They cannot even trust God. For alcoholism destroys self-confidence.

"Tell me," I said. "Have you ever shared with another person the fact that you have a drinking problem?" Her eyes simply flashed defiance at me. I could tell she was thinking I was terribly stupid to ask that question.

"Of course not!" she said. "I don't talk about the bad things in my life with anyone else."

"Then how do you expect others to help if you are unwilling to share what's troubling you?" I said. "Sharing the load will make your burden much lighter. In fact there is no therapy more helpful than finding a person you can trust and then talking things out."

"But my problems are personal. I don't want to talk to everyone about them," she said.

"You're right. You shouldn't," I said. "But there is a big difference in talking about your problems to just anyone and sharing your load with a trusted person or friend.''

I suggested to her that she choose one friend or member of the family and let that person know that he or she had been specifically selected for a very special reason—to share a very important concern. Then Mary should try to explain to this person what she was going through and how she really felt about it.

I can still hear her saying, ''But every time I share something personal with someone, I always get hurt. They use it against me.''

Most people, unfortunately, find it easier to share a problem with those they don't respect or admire, I pointed out. And as a result they end up being disappointed.

''When you're trying to get off alcohol, you need to be careful in whom you put your trust. Just as a diseased person can infect others, so can individuals who suffer from sick thinking spread germs to the very people who ask them for help,'' I said. ''Fortunately those who have made a recovery from a drinking problem themselves can also infect you with the kind of thinking that brings about recovery.''

Then I asked Mary to look back and see if the person with whom she had shared her problems had been the right person, someone who was trustworthy and reliable.

''You know, you are right,'' said Mary. ''The only people to whom I've ever talked about my troubles have been drunks themselves! And they had no intention of changing, either. I never considered talking to people who have done something constructive about their own drinking problem.''

''Pick out the best person you know, someone you admire and who is in the best position to help you,'' I said. ''Do you know anyone who has found sobriety and made a complete change of life-style?'' Mary searched her memory. Suddenly her face lit up.

''Yes, I do, and she's a lovely person,'' Mary said. ''Jane

and I were in the same sorority years ago. Both of us had drinking problems even then, though we didn't realize it.

"A few years ago Jane did something to get off alcohol. At least once or twice she said something to me about my drinking. But when she mentioned that, I stopped seeing her," Mary said.

"Perhaps you would like to call Jane now and ask if you could come by and visit her," I suggested, handing her the telephone. I knew that Mary had been to other counselors and ministers and even to some doctors. She needed all these helpers, but it was evident she needed to develop a satisfying relationship with another person too. But now Mary seemed to be hesitating.

"Is something wrong?" I asked. With her head bowed and eyes searching the floor, this woman who had appeared to be so independent said in a very fearful, timid voice, "But what will I say to her?"

"You're doing a wonderful job of expressing yourself to me," I pointed out. "Talk to her the same way. Remember she has already mentioned your drinking problem to you. I'm sure she did that because she wanted to help you, not harm you.

"You might start the conversation off by thanking her for thinking about you," I suggested. Many alcoholics, I knew, need to recognize the genuine concern which others have for them. They must realize that others want to reach out to them, not criticize them.

"Mary, you are the one who has to let your sorority sister know you need her help. You have to open the door so that Jane can walk in. If you do, I am sure that Jane will be open to you," I said. "But the real question is 'Do you really want help?' "

"I do want help," Mary said, "but I don't want others to know I have a drinking problem."

"But you haven't been able to keep your drinking a secret. People already know," I pointed out. "Perhaps the reason you have not asked others to come to your aid or have not joined some supportive group is that you do not want to commit yourself."

Mary needed to realize that it was only too natural for people to pay attention to the things she had done wrong as opposed to her good and worthwhile accomplishments. The only way she could change their impressions of her now was by changing her own attitude and behavior first. She had to extend herself and ask for the kind of experiences she would like to receive.

When I was a small boy working for a farmer, the old man and I used to round up the cows in the evening. Every time one of us would yell at the cows, we could hear our voices echoing in the hills. I will never forget the farmer's observing, "Whatever you say will come back to you in life." How true are his words!

"If you are willing to commit yourself to getting help and finding a new life, then call Jane," I said. "At the right moment, explain to her that you would like some help. Let her know you have been sober for a few days, but that sobriety never lasts any longer for you.

"Tell her that you need her to share with you how she has been able to stay sober. Let her know that you would like all the support and help she can give—even if it is nothing more than just a kind word or a bit of attention."

Even though it was extremely hard for Mary to admit to Jane that she had a drinking problem, she did call her and ask for help. She found Jane was only too glad to respond. In fact Mary's friend had wanted to help her for a long time. But she had felt cut off from Mary because of her attempt to cover up the problem and pretend it was not there.

I know it is only too natural to put off asking others to help even in simple matters. How many times have we driven our automobiles to a strange place, looking for a certain street? Even when we know we are lost and can't locate the address, we keep trying to find it by ourselves. We drive around in circles, making the same mistakes over and over. How reluctant we are to stop and ask for directions!

When we are first learning to play golf, few of us would refuse to ask for instructions on how to swing the club or master the game. Yet we often struggle along in life's more important contests, putting aside opportunities for expertise.

Don't be ashamed or afraid to ask others to help you. People are still real. They can help us back on our feet. No one walks an easy road, but by establishing a right relationship with another human being the journey can be made easier.

Without love and friendship to keep us going, our hearts wither, and our spirits droop. Walking together, each sharing the strength of the other, we can conquer the highest mountain.

5

Pitfalls on the Road to Recovery

Three weeks after Dick and I had committed his older brother, Bill, to the hospital, I telephoned Dick.

"How does Bill seem to be getting along?" I asked. I knew that Bill had just about finished the period required for detoxification and physical rehabilitation. I also knew that Dick had seen his brother at this point in his recovery many times before. I was hoping this would be the last hospital stay for Bill, but I could hear Dick sigh over the phone.

"He's like always," said Dick. "He can hardly wait to be released so that he can get home to his wife, his children, and his job. He wants to make up for all that lost time.

"You know," continued Dick, "Bill's like a golfer who finds himself in the rough. He can't wait to play the next shot because he just knows he won't dub it again. But somehow he always does; he just ends up in another trap."

There was a painful silence on the line between us for a moment, and then Dick said, "You would think Bill would learn from his mistakes, but he never seems to."

After three weeks in the hospital, Bill's physical system had made a remarkable recovery. Now Bill felt he had to correct all the mistakes he ever had made. He had to catch up in his work, because his job was threatened and his bills delinquent.

44

From experience in working with alcoholics, I knew that it takes one to two years for full recovery to be realized. After all, it took Bill years to deteriorate. There just was no hope of undoing all that damage in a short period of time. It takes patience and commitment to get sober.

Bill just hadn't taken to heart Alcoholics Anonymous' wonderful slogan: "Easy does it." Most people in trouble with alcohol move from one extreme to another. It was apparent that Bill was again going to fall into the trap of trying to accomplish too much too soon. He would overtax himself mentally, physically, and spiritually. Soon he would be as nervous, anxious, and depressed as before.

I knew that Bill would not have had time to learn to follow the new, healthy routines to which he had barely been exposed. With all the tension he was going to create for himself, I felt sure Bill would return to drinking. Alcohol had been the only method he had for dealing with stress.

But trying to do too much too soon is only one of the many pitfalls that lurk on the road to recovery. In this chapter I hope to put up some big red highway warning signs describing the detours, roadblocks, and dangerous curves you may experience in your own journey to a healthier life.

A common mistake for recovering alcoholics is to believe that someone or some particular program will keep them sober. It may sound harsh, but there is nothing that will get people sober or keep them sober except confinement in a place where no alcohol is available.

Dick can't keep Bill sober; neither can Bill's wife or children. There is no pill that will keep him from taking a drink. Alcoholics Anonymous can't keep him away from the bottle. God won't do it for him—neither can the preacher or the church.

Granted, there are any number of plans which Bill can follow to help him get sober and stay that way. But Bill must work the plan. It can't be done for him.

Bill's wife can put a recipe for a cake on the kitchen sink. It can stay there from now on, but no cake will appear unless she follows the recipe. She must measure the ingredients, mix the batter, set the oven, and bake the cake before her family can have it for dessert. She has to work the plan.

Whatever plan Bill chooses from the many that are available, he must be committed to it. He must put his best efforts into making the plan work. Most of the time it is not the program that does not work, but the person who fails to work the program.

How often have I heard persons in trouble with alcohol complain: "God hasn't helped me. The church hasn't kept me sober"!

It is true that God will not make the program work for a person. Every athlete needs a coach who will give directions and a program, but it is up to the player to master the routines. The athlete must be committed to the program. The same is true with persons recovering from alcoholism. God will not make the program work, but He can give strength and courage to help them master the routines they must learn. There simply is no way of producing a crop we have never planted and nurtured!

Other pitfalls come in the guise of people who think they are helping the recovering alcoholic. They mean well, but they are spoilers for those who are trying to get sober and stay sober.

Bill was fortunate in having family, friends, and fellow workers who all were supporting and encouraging him. Others may not be as lucky. Their "helpers" may actually discourage them from trying to stay on a program that leads to recovery.

I knew one lady who, after years of trouble with her drinking problem, made the commitment to join Alcoholics Anonymous. But what a struggle she had to follow the plan!

What odds she had to work against! Her husband made fun of her. He laughed at her commitment.

"She doesn't have to attend all those meetings!" he would say. "All she has to do is stop drinking." On the nights she was to attend, he would come home late from the office or simply refuse to care for the children. He would not attend any of the open meetings of Alcoholics Anonymous with her. Nor would he go to the Al-Anon groups. He simply had no intentions of trying to understand his wife's problems or the program she was trying to follow.

"I'm not about to meet with a bunch of drunks," he said, in spite of his wife's pleas to attend.

Other walking and talking pitfalls are those people who pressure the recovering alcoholic to drink.

"Come on, one little drink won't hurt," says one.

"Have a beer," says another. "That couldn't cause any trouble."

"This is a very special occasion," insists a third. "You can't let us celebrate alone."

Such words are always inviting. When someone offers you a drink, recognize his good intentions, but refuse it. Let him know you mean what you say. You can be kind in declining, but be firm and determined not to take that first drink.

Often you can redirect your friend's efforts to be hospitable by merely saying, "No thank you. I don't care to have a beer, but I would like a Coke."

Strange though it may seem, people who offer you a drink are showing concern for you. Therefore, you can express your gratefulness for their intentions but turn their concern into something constructive rather than destructive. You are in control. You can call the shots.

You must realize that many other people look on drinking together as a token of friendship. Your refusal to drink seems like rejection, unless you let them know it is not.

Then there are others who feel they cannot drink unless you join them. If you let it be known clearly that it is all right with you if they drink while you sip a Coke, the pressure will usually be dropped.

But whatever you do, *don't* wait until a drink is offered to make the decision about how you will respond. If you are not prepared, you will likely make the wrong decision.

One very big pitfall for recovering alcoholics is the desire to turn away from life. Most alcoholics just naturally seem to do more than their share of worrying. They have used alcohol to escape the demands, troubles, duties, and worries that occur naturally to anyone who lives in this old world.

If you are a recovering alcoholic, it is perfectly normal for you to want to withdraw from others for a while. You want to "get hold of yourself," relax, and regroup.

What you must now learn to do is to leave the past behind and deal with the future one day at a time. Trying to live tomorrow today is dangerous. Besides, it can't be done! You must learn to do one job at a time. For you the number-one priority is that of staying sober. Decide what is most important; then give it all you have.

But how do you stop living in the past with its weekly grocery list of regrets that leave you depleted of energy for the living of a single day? When pent-up emotions build to the point of explosion, physical exercise can calm you down. Get out and take a walk, go for a swim, mow the lawn, play a game of golf or tennis. Or go visit with a friend; talk to someone you admire.

Beware of the pitfall of being a perfectionist. Most alcoholics cannot tolerate anything being less than perfect. There is nothing wrong with wanting to do a good job. But do not expect too much from yourself. No one else expects you to be perfect. Learn to do the best you can and leave the rest to life. Learn to accept your skills and abilities for what they are.

I don't mean that you should not try to improve your skills and abilities. Like a pole-vaulter training for the Olympics, you should set your goals high enough to make you reach for new records—but not so high that you ruin your chances of making the team. The important thing is to make sure your motives are right. All of us are human and limited in what we can do.

Even food can be a pitfall to the recovering alcoholic. If you are hungry or fatigued, not only your stomach feels discomfort. Your mind suffers too. It is especially true for the recovering alcoholic that if you get too hungry you are likely to become depressed. Good, nourishing meals improve not only your physical strength, but your mental outlook as well. Eat regularly to conquer inner tensions.

The pitfalls of hate, anger, and guilt can't actually be seen as faulty stage props in the drama of the recovering alcoholic; but they are always there. We express hate by resentment, hostility, and grudges. These emotions, triggered by our experiences, can cause actual chemical changes in the body. They will leave you "all tied up in knots."

This pitfall has always been another of Bill's biggest problems. Every time someone says or does something which hurts him—or even if he just remembers a painful experience in the past—he feels "all done in." Bill always remembers his hurts and never thinks of the compliments people have given him. He remembers failures, not accomplishments.

Why did this have to happen to me? Bill always asks himself when he feels hurt. He never thinks to question himself, *What could I do to bring about a change in my behavior that would make things better?*

Everything doesn't have to be perfect. Our problems

don't have to be completely solved before we can start reacting to hurts in a different way. Bill may not be able to change the way his wife nags at him in front of other people; of course it would be easier for him if she would compliment him instead. But since that is not likely to happen, he will have to find ways to deal constructively with his feelings.

Far too many of us are too proud, too easily hurt. We wear our feelings on our sleeves. We are too sensitive. Bill must learn to find the inner freedom which comes from forgiveness and understanding—the same forgiveness others have extended to him.

All of us must do a lot of overlooking of faults and forgetting too, if we are not to be tripped up in the pitfalls of anger. There is no way to get rid of hate without the spirit of forgiveness.

When you feel that someone has failed you, and you recognize hate beginning to tighten the bonds around you, ask the simple question, *What could I have done differently to have made things better?*

It helps, when you feel angry or hurt, to do something positive. But you have to expend actual effort for others, not just think positively. Go out of your way to do something good for another person. You get a double benefit. You have the warm feeling that comes from helping another person. At the same time, your actions take your mind off yourself. You can cope with your emotions. You won't have to take that drink.

Leisure time can be a pitfall too. Drinking takes a lot of hours out of the week. When you are an alcoholic, there is little time left to do anything else. When Bill stopped drinking, he found he had time on his hands. He needed to become active in Alcoholics Anonymous and the church. Not only would he find a constructive program to follow; he would also find a new social life. And that is very important!

He needed to rub shoulders with others who have found their way in life.

Don't wait for others to find you. Take the initiative in making friends and in getting involved in something worthwhile. "Seek and you will find."

If you don't handle your time, it will handle you. Just as you plan your workday, also plan your leisure time. The biggest pitfall of all is having leisure time with nothing to do.

Still another pitfall is not being flexible. Learn to bend like a reed so that you will not break under the hurricane winds of everyday life. I once saw very graphically how rigid stone will chip very easily while even the thinnest sheet of flexible rubber will withstand great pressure. A workman once sandblasted the letters of our church's name into a stone. He used a very thin piece of rubber to outline each letter; then he blasted away. The hard, rigid rock was quickly indented. But the areas covered by the thin sheet of rubber withstood the pressure and left the stone underneath raised in the shape of letters. You too must learn the art of giving and receiving so that you will not break under the pressures of everyday life.

The temptation to drink is an ever-present pitfall. You should, for that reason, eliminate as many reminders of alcohol as possible. One alcoholic with whom I was working seemed forever to have his "slips." One day, as I was riding with him in his car, I heard something rolling around in his trunk.

"What in the world is making all that noise?" I finally asked.

"Oh, that?" the man replied. "That's a fifth of whiskey. I always keep it in my trunk so that when I hear it roll around I know I can have a drink whenever I want it. You can never get away from liquor anyway; so you might just as well learn to live with it."

"You're right about not being able to get away from

liquor," I said. "But there is enough temptation in magazine ads and well-meaning friends' invitations to drink, as it is. Why do you intentionally tempt yourself with the sound of a fifth of whiskey rolling around in your trunk?"

"But I've always carried a fifth back there. If I remove it now, to me that would be a sign of weakness," he argued.

"Are you sure? Or would it be good, common sense to remove it?" I asked. "The last five slips you have had were rough ones. Where did you get the alcohol for each of those first drinks?" He looked a little shamefaced then.

"You know, I never thought of it that way before. I got them from the bottle I carried around in the trunk of my car." Right that minute he stopped the car, opened the trunk, and poured out the fifth of whiskey at the side of the road.

Later he told me, "You will never know what a help that was to me. What a temptation I was fighting every time I heard that bottle roll around!"

Not all temptations can be removed, of course. Instead of trying to flee from all of them or attempting to rely on some superhuman strength of your own, you should develop a good offense. Surround yourself with the bulwarks of Alcoholics Anonymous, the church, and other groups who will offer the companionship of people who fully understand. They can give you a sense of belonging, of being needed and wanted.

As the days pass and these groups provide all kinds of help, you will gain new strength. You will find new experiences devoid of temptations to drink. Certainly you cannot remove every temptation, but you can replace the snares along your pathway with protective fences. When new relationships and social structures have been established, no longer will the temptation to drink be so strong.

This is by no means the entire list of pitfalls on the road to recovery. Pitfalls are very individual experiences. They vary from person to person.

If you have experienced slips on the road to recovery, ask yourself these questions: *When did it happen? Where did it happen? What was the circumstance? What was the emotion? What could I have done to prevent it from happening?*

Take time to write down what happened and how you dealt with it. Try to find out what triggered your trouble. What was your pitfall? Then, when you find out what it is, don't try to overcome it alone.

6

What to Do About Overloads

A young man in a shiny, well-cared-for pickup truck drove up to a huge mountain of sand on a construction site. As he started loading the pickup with the sand, shovelful by shovelful, a group of sidewalk superintendents soon gathered.

"You'd better be careful, son," said one of them. "That sand is heavy. You're liable to overload your truck." The young man laughed.

"Don't worry, this truck was built with an extra-big capacity, and it can handle anything. It has overloads to take care of the weight," he said. But as he continued shoveling, the bed of the pickup moved closer and closer to the ground. Finally the springs were resting on the overload, and they gave way.

"I told you so," the older man said.

The owner of the truck scratched his head. "I don't understand," he said. "My truck is constructed to take loads that are heavier than other pickups can take. I've loaded it that heavy lots of times before."

"Maybe," said the whittling bystander, "you overloaded it so many times that the stress just built up. Today's load was the final straw."

"I guess I'll just have to unload it then," said the young man. But after several shovelfuls, it was apparent that he would need to call for help. The overloads had given way completely. He could not repair the damage he had done.

Like the young man's truck, most alcoholics can usually handle more alcohol than the average person without showing too many undesirable effects. Their systems just seem to have a way of handling large quantities, almost as if they had overloads built into them. With their physical predisposition and higher tolerance for alcohol than other people, they become confident in their ability to handle lots of liquor.

The young man who was so proud of his pickup with overloads believed firmly that he could shovel in as much sand as he wished. He had been doing just that for so long that he was no longer even conscious that he was overloading.

Individuals who drink have a tendency to do the same thing. Eventually they overload their systems—both nervous and organic—too many times. Just as the pickup finally broke under the weight, they find it doesn't take much of an additional drink to break down their systems completely.

The young man learned the hard way that if he continued to overload his pickup, he would not only damage the springs that carry the load, but he would ruin the motor too. And people who drink too much not only hurt their organs and nervous system. They eventually damage the motor that drives everything—their brain.

It is at this point that alcoholics suddenly realize the need to unload. But even when they do, by becoming sober, they still find it is difficult to function because of the damage which has been done.

What can one do? The man with the pickup did a very wise thing. He called for help, because he realized he did not know the first thing about repairing his truck. But to whom did he turn, and how did he know he was going to find the right person?

The first thing this young man did was to ask those who

were standing around if they had ever been involved in a similar situation, and if so, who fixed their trucks.

One man said, "I tell you what I did. I got me a book on mechanics. I studied it and worked it out. Nothing to it."

Perhaps this is one way that you can help yourself, but you should be forewarned that very few persons ever do learn to live a healthy life on their own. If you want to learn about alcoholism, there are materials that you can read and study that will help you understand what is happening. But most of the time when individuals try to stay sober on their own, they are not happy in their sobriety. There seems to be something lacking. Besides, doing it alone is the most difficult way to help yourself. Fixing a broken pickup is not a simple matter for the average person. It's also harder to learn to stay sober and live a normal life without some help.

And just as a game of golf is more fun if you play with someone rather than alone, so is the road to sobriety made more pleasant and healthier if it is traveled with others.

The young man knew he didn't want to try to repair the pickup himself, so he asked those standing around what they thought he ought to do. He found that while everyone was sympathetic, each had a different opinion about how to approach the problem. There was no agreement on the solution.

You too might want to discuss the matter frankly with those who are around you. I am sure that many of them will be understanding concerning your problem, though they may not agree as to what the solution is. But you probably should talk to your family about your drinking. They need to know that you realize that you have overloaded your system and want some kind of help.

The young man then did a smart thing. After discussing the broken overloads with those around him, he called a professional mechanic. This expert had training. He understood the problem thoroughly and knew just how to fix it.

You too, perhaps, should talk to the professionals. A

doctor should be consulted, because you may have physical needs that only a medical expert can understand. Call your minister, because there is no doubt that the spiritual dimension of your life has been greatly damaged by the overload.

When the young man did bring a mechanic to the scene of his broken pickup, this expert immediately realized that there was no way it could be repaired on the spot. So a wrecker was brought to tow it to the garage.

It may be that people who have overloaded their systems with alcohol can no longer find help from those around them. They may need to go to the hospital, the drug center, or some other place where the right kind of care can be given while repairs are being made. In almost every community now there are rehabilitation centers, detoxification centers, and hospitals that care very well for alcoholics.

There was a time when alcoholics could legitimately excuse themselves from such treatment becuse of the cost, but that day is past now. In every community there are facilities available that almost anyone can afford. Many insurance policies now cover treatment. The great stumbling block is that most individuals do not want to call for help. They have a great fear of treatment.

But do not be afraid, and don't put off calling for assistance. All you have to do is contact those in your community who know about alcohol centers. They can give you the information you need. Your minister or doctor can help in such matters.

Another source in almost every community now is Alcoholics Anonymous. This group has helped untold numbers of people who have "unloaded" their systems and found themselves able to live a new life. It has achieved an unbelievable record in rehabilitating alcoholics.

This wonderful fellowship began in 1935 through the efforts of two alcoholics, Broker Bill and Doctor Bob, who got together believing there had to be a better way than any then available to help each other remain sober. Now its

membership has become worldwide. Those who band
themselves together in AA seem to have a sense of joy and
happiness that is a marvel to outsiders.

No doubt their attitude stems from the fact that they soon
discover they are not freaks or unique phenomena. There
are others with the same problems, who are not only willing
to help but to share their own feelings of helplessness, loneliness, and fear. The emotional and social deprivation that
all alcoholics have suffered in the past causes them to understand each other and form a strong union.

There are no dues or fees required to be a part of AA. It
has one purpose only—to help alcoholics recover. AA
members do this by surrounding alcoholics with love, understanding, and concern while giving them the help they
need to stop drinking and to stay off alcohol. AA's program
is not based on past mistakes but on what the member can
accomplish today.

AA has two allied groups, Al-Anon and Alateen. These
organizations aid families, relatives, friends, and children of
problem drinkers.

Because alcoholism has a tremendous emotional impact
upon the immediate family, these relatives may themselves
become so emotionally upset that they are inadequate to
help their loved one or live meaningful lives of their own. In
Al-Anon families of alcoholics learn that their best defense
against the emotional impact of alcoholism is gaining
knowledge and achieving the maturity and courage needed
to put that knowledge into effect.

Alateen is for teenagers and preteens who wish to learn
how to cope with the troubles brought about by alcoholism
within their families.

If you are interested in finding out more about one of
these programs, you may attend one of the many open
meetings of AA, Al-Anon, and Alateen. All three groups
follow AA's Twelve Steps as the basis of their program. But
these Twelve Steps will create different challenges and

growth for every alcoholic and his or her family.

Here are the Twelve Steps and the way in which a typical member of AA, Al-Anon, or Alateen uses them in different ways to achieve a healthier life.

Step One   We admitted we were powerless over alcohol—that our lives had become unmanageable.

Step Two   Came to believe that a Power greater than ourselves could restore us to sanity.

Step Three   Made a decision to turn our will and our lives over to the care of God *as we understood Him.*

Step Four   Made a searching and fearless moral inventory of ourselves.

Step Five   Admitted to God, to ourselves, and to another human being the exact nature of our wrongs.

Step Six   Were entirely ready to have God remove all these defects of character.

Step Seven   Humbly asked Him to remove our shortcomings.

Step Eight   Made a list of all persons we had harmed, and became willing to make amends to them all.

Step Nine   Made direct amends to such people wherever possible, except where to do so would injure them or others.

Step Ten   Continued to take personal inventory and when we were wrong, promptly admitted it.

Step Eleven   Sought through prayer and meditation to improve our conscious contact with God *as we understood Him,* praying only for knowledge of His will for us and the power to carry that out.

Step Twelve   Having had a spiritual awakening as a result of these steps, we tried to carry this message to alcoholics, and to practice these principles in all our affairs.

The alcoholic has reached the point where he is power-less over alcohol. While it is difficult for anyone to admit complete defeat, the acceptance of his powerlessness is the first step in liberation from alcohol. The disease of al-coholism results from a combination of a mental obsession to drink and an increasing sensitivity to alcohol which amounts to a physical allergy. Therefore self-confidence in managing his drinking becomes a liability rather than an asset.

In the past it was thought that only the most desperate alcoholics—those who had "hit bottom"—could bring themselves to admit this powerlessness. Today, with the help of AA, even young people who are as yet only poten-tial alcoholics have been able to "bottom out" at an early stage in their drinking and declare this powerlessness.

Since the alcoholic is powerless to be rid of the alcohol obsession, some Higher Power must necessarily do it. AA does not demand belief. It only requires an open mind to-ward the possibility that there is a Higher Power. For some, the belief in the ability of AA to help is sufficient as a beginning.

Following Step Two requires a completely different path for the agnostic or atheist than for the person who once had faith but lost it, or who still believes but finds faith no pro-tection from alcohol. In following this step, the AA member learns the importance of positive thinking and the necessity of fighting the problems of intellectuality, self-sufficiency, and self-righteousness. True humility and an open mind can lead to faith. Every AA meeting is an assurance that God will restore him to sanity if he rightly relates himself to Him.

How does the alcoholic let God into his life? Step Three is like opening a locked door to the kingdom, using his willingness as the key. He learns to become dependent as a means to independence.

Through an inventory of himself the alcoholic seeks to discover the liabilities in himself which have brought him to physical, moral, and spiritual bankruptcy. It is difficult for him to overcome his rationalizing and extreme feelings of guilt. The help of an AA sponsor can avoid the situation in which the sufferer makes a misguided moral inventory which can result in guilt, grandiosity, or blaming others.

Even with this inventory these conflicts still are not ended. To solve the deadly business of living alone with his conflicts, the alcoholic must confess these wrongs to God and another human being. He gives a fearless admission of his defects to his AA sponsor, a trusted minister, or a professional worker; in return he receives forgiveness and learns to give it to others. Confession is the beginning of true kinship between God and man. The oneness with God prepares the alcoholic for further growth through the rest of the steps.

Many alcoholics balk at Step Six because they do not wish to have all their defects of character removed; this is because, like most people, they love their flaws too much. But they can quit their stubborn, rebellious hanging on to them. Each one can say, "This I cannot do today, but I will stop crying out, 'No, never!' " Any person who is capable of enough willingness and honesty to try this step on all his faults—without any reservations whatever—has indeed come a long way spiritually and is sincerely trying to grow in the image and likeness of his own Creator.

This confession leads naturally to the next step, humility before God. Humility is a desire to seek and to do God's will rather than our striving for our own happiness. Step Seven leads the alcoholic to true freedom of the human spirit, because it permits him to move out of himself and toward God. The alcoholic learns that God can turn his weaknessess into His strengths if he is willing to have Him remove his shortcomings, as God wills to do it, under the conditions of the day he asks.

The alcoholic begins the fascinating adventure of learning to live with others. In making a list of persons he has harmed, he must overcome the obstacles of being reluctant to forgive those whom he has hurt; of refusing to see the wrongs he has done to others, even those who have harmed him; of purposeful forgetting.

He makes good on his willingness to make amends by learning to speak frankly with those whom he has seriously affected, except when it would injure them or other people. He must even make amends to those persons who were not at all aware of what he has done to them. He must be ready to take responsibility for the well-being of others. Timing is important.

Can the alcoholic stay sober and keep his emotional balance under all conditions? He learns to make self-searching a regular habit, to admit, accept, and patiently correct his defects. As he makes a daily inventory of his shortcomings, he learns also to celebrate his constructive behavior.

Learning to meditate is a different experience for each individual, yet all will find the light of God's reality, the nourishment of His strength, and the atmosphere of His grace. After opening a channel to God through meditation, the alcoholic prays by asking for those right things of which he and others are in the greatest need. He learns not to ask for the changes that he thinks should be made, for he is not God, but that "Thy will, not mine, be done" in all situations.

When he has received a spiritual awakening, he is transformed, because he has laid hold of a source of strength which formerly was denied him. Finding himself in possession of a degree of honesty, tolerance, unselfishness, peace of mind, and love, of which he had thought himself quite incapable, he is able to turn outward toward his fellow alcoholics who are still in distress. He practices the Twelve

Steps within his family, at work, and wherever he is. The wonderful energy which the Twelfth Step releases and the eager action by which it carries the message to others are the magnificent reality of AA.

The family, affected by the life-style of the alcoholic, must learn to deal with its own problems as well as understanding those of the alcoholic. In Step One the nonalcoholic is freed from the often-held fear that he is sometimes responsible for the alcoholic's drinking. With full acceptance of his powerlessness over the disease of alcoholism, he has a feeling of release. Hope returns. The nonalcoholic member of the family can turn his full attention to the managing of his own life and bringing it into some sort of order. When even one member of the family is thinking sanely, the whole group situation improves.

Before he had help from Al-Anon the nonalcoholic had reached a point where he was no longer reacting normally. Since in fear and insane dread he was no longer able to command himself, he had to turn to a Higher Power for emotional stability. He must make a conscious, wholehearted bending and merging of his energies with God's will. Everything is directed in orderly progression instead of in chaotic confusion. He learns he must be constantly reaffirming and renewing his decision until the temptation to use his own will gradually disappears.

The family learns to be completely honest with each other, each realizing that he has not always been the one who was entirely right. The nonalcoholic discovers that he has held grudges, been overly sensitive, too easily hurt, or selfish. He learns to forgive and pray for the other person.

By admitting wrongs, the family moves in the direction of a healthy, sharing attitude toward life. By putting themselves on record, they can overcome liabilities which are holding them back.

By being ready to have character defects removed, the

nonalcoholic makes himself receptive to God's help and becomes willing to let God change him as He will. He becomes conscious of the need for a Power greater than himself and a willingness to let that Power control his life. He realizes that most of his failings are habits he has allowed himself to form and keep. He will probably never be perfect, but with His help he can be less imperfect.

The family comes to realize that each member can no longer solve his discontent by putting it on the shoulders of others. In making a list of persons he has harmed, the family member may find the person he has harmed most is himself. If he has harmed the family through neglect, ill-temper, or harsh treatment, a change in attitude, conscientiously pursued, may counteract the injuries. Sometimes he can make amends by accepting his share of the work outside the home and in the community, which he may have been avoiding through past embarrassment.

As all human beings, the family members realize they will continue to make their share of mistakes. Frequent inventories evaluate their progress and show them how they can avoid future wrong.

The family must not argue about what God's will is, but must try to come closer to the Higher Power through meditation and prayer. The members each must learn that they don't have to understand His will completely to follow it.

With the Twelfth Step the family's spiritual growth is unlimited and their rewards are endless as each tries to bring the message of the Twelve Steps to others and live it in every phase of his existence.

The teenager learns that he is powerless over alcohol and that the problem is not his to solve, but the alcoholic's. Before Alateen the young person's life had become unmanageable. The only life he can change is his own.

He must look for a Power greater than his own to help him. It is important for him to realize that there is a Power beyond his own understanding. This Power does not force His will on mankind. The decision to accept Him or reject Him is up to each individual. Making a decision may be hard for some, easy for others. The teenager must believe that doing God's will is a dependable way to be truly happy.

A young person must try to look at himself objectively with the help of the Higher Power, to remember he has good qualities as well as faults, to be completely honest with himself. He cannot blame his faults on others. These faults really do exist; the young person must face them objectively. This step helps to develop honesty, humility, and straight thinking.

At this point it is time to do something about his character defects. Each person must be willing to have God take them away and replace them with good, honest thoughts and actions that are His will. This may not appeal to anyone at first. The teenager may feel that he would rather do it himself, or that God can't or won't help him. But he has to admit that when he was living on his own, he didn't do so well. God will help him by giving him the strength to do the right thing. It's up to him to try.

In listing people, the teenager may often think of people he has hurt whom he felt had also hurt him. He must not be concerned with what they did to him, but with what he did to them. Now he must admit that there is no excuse for taking out his emotions on others.

The phrase "I'm sorry" is only one approach to apology. There will be some people to whom only partial amends can be made. A frank review of the situation might do more harm than good to the others involved. In some cases action should be postponed, or the situation should never be reopened at all.

The teenager must continue to take personal inventory and find which defects are giving him the most trouble. Promptly admitting when he is wrong becomes a continuing practice in humility. He achieves growing peace of mind and serenity because he is able to see that he is making progress. His personal worth increases as he gains insight and stops being afraid to make mistakes.

Through prayer the teenager can get to know what God wants him to do. That means he has to think over his problems and talk to God about them. It means he has to think about God and try to apply his new insights to his daily life. Faith in God's love will help him to love himself and accept His will for him. He must believe that whatever He asks of him, God will give him the strength to do.

7

Alcoholism
Is a Family Problem

For the first time in months, Sally walked into my office with a spring in her step. Her eyes sparkled instead of being clouded over with sadness. She even laughed and joked with my secretary. I knew that something good had happened.

"Bill hasn't had a drink in a solid month!" she burst out.

"That's wonderful," I said. "Has he found someone to help him?"

"Oh, you know how stubborn Bill is," Sally said. "He just won't go to AA or a psychiatrist or anyone else. But that's why I'm so proud of him. He just quit drinking all by himself."

When Sally said that, my hopes for her were dashed. Just because Bill had quit drinking, Bill's and Sally's problems would not disappear. In fact I knew from experience that quite the opposite was likely.

Alcoholism is a family problem, one that is shared by husband, wife, and children. Members are not cured of this painful disease simply because the alcoholic reaches sobriety.

Can any member of a family experience the anxiety, the unhealed wounds, the physical deterioration, the destruction of family ties, the loss of confidence and trust, and all the other hurts that go along with alcohol abuse—and not be affected?

Yes, it is true that alcoholism is an illness. But it is one which has a great emotional effect upon the family. All the members have made a mutual adaptation to the drinking. Many times they become just as sick as the alcoholic.

The more distorted the emotions of the alcoholic's next of kin become, the less adequate will be the help which relatives can give their troubled loved one.

As a result, what family members do before and after sobriety is reached may become destructive rather than supportive, no matter how hard they try.

I could not help remembering what fourteen-year-old Bill, Jr., had told me when I tried to get him involved with the youth group.

"I don't want to make any new friends," he said. "And even if I found some people I liked, I wouldn't let them come to my house and hear our family fights. Dad's always drinking, and Mom's always nagging. Besides, Dad doesn't like me, so he wouldn't like my friends, either. He's always on my back, accusing me of smoking pot, stealing, or taking dope. He has even told me I'm not really his son. No, I just don't want any friends at all."

Now that Bill's dad had quit drinking, would those feelings disappear? I knew they could not—not without help. Child abuse, whether it is verbal or physical, and exposure to the alcoholic personality create youngsters who feel they are unworthy. Because of their poor self-image, they are easily confused and frustrated. Often they do poorly in school. They refuse to try to relate to their peers, because they are afraid of failure. And they are far more likely to suffer maladjustment than children who do not live in such an environment.

In fact they have a far greater chance of becoming alcoholics themselves, or becoming addicted to another chemical, than children who have grown up without this problem.

When a family member stops drinking, the husband, the wife, and the children too must learn to adapt to the fact that there is no longer an alcoholic in the household. This change is more difficult than it might seem. The problem is that often the spouse and children blame the alcoholic for all the problems that have existed, while the alcoholic is insisting it is the family that caused his drinking. The entire family must be willing to change its attitude and outlook toward the alcoholic member. All must be able to take a careful look at their own behavior and the responsibility they will have to take for that behavior.

Family members will have to accept new roles if they are to heal themselves and function together as a family. Both the alcoholics and their kin need a treatment program which they can follow simultaneously.

I knew that it would be far better for Sally, Bill, and Bill, Jr., too if Sally realized that the basic problem she faced was one of gaining knowledge and then achieving the emotional maturity and courage necessary to live in a new way. With her lack of knowledge, Sally helped her husband avoid treatment.

Even though Bill would not seek assistance for himself, Sally could have speeded his recovery if she had reached out for aid. She did not realize that members of the family are too close to each other, too emotionally involved, to help treat the illness of alcoholism. Her only hope for not playing into the progressive-illness pattern of her alcoholic husband—and thereby hastening his decline—was to find assistance for herself.

But instead Sally believed Bill's sobriety solved everything for the whole family. Since Sally didn't see any need for coming to church any longer, she dropped out. So did Bill and Bill, Jr. I didn't see Sally for a long time.

Three years later she visited my office once again, and I was shocked at her appearance. Her eyes no longer sparkled. In fact she looked as if her whole world had caved in. She dabbed a tissue to her eyes and poured out her wretched story: Bill, Sr., was still completely sober, but he was making life miserable. Bill, Jr., was on drugs.

"It sounds terrible, I know, but I almost wish Bill were drinking again. When he was mean and ugly to me, I could blame it on alcohol. And, at least, when he sobered up he treated me like a queen, because he felt guilty.

"But now that he's not drinking, he is cruel and selfish all the time. He's just no good, and I've lost all respect for him."

While Bill had stopped drinking, he was not really sober in the true sense of the word. He was uncomfortable and unhappy without alcohol. There had been no constructive change in the attitude and behavior of either Bill or Sally.

I saw that both had continued to be very immature. Bill was easily bored, disorganized, and destructive. With his feelings fluctuating, he was likely to fly into a rage at a moment's notice over practically nothing.

Bill simply was unable to see himself as others saw him. He was convinced that he could do no wrong—that whenever life became unpleasant it was because he was a victim of circumstances beyond his control. Without alcohol, he was once again the center of many of the family's grievances.

Sally's reactions ranged from discouragement to confusion, depression, resentfulness, and bitterness.

Both Bill and Sally were unable to appreciate the aspects of life that mature people often enjoy. They seldom did anything together. They were not sensitive to one another's feelings. In fact they were unable to communicate with each other.

They had no goals, no purpose, in their lives. Their enthusiasms were often juvenile in duration and intensity.

Dissatisfaction seemed to be their constant state. This family was a disaster for parents and child.

Other families have different problems from those Bill and Sally experienced with alcoholism. Yet no alcoholics can be viewed alone as suffering individuals apart from their own flesh and blood and those around them.

It is simply unbelievable how the alcoholic plays one relative off against another, and how the family in turn manipulates the drinking person. The alcoholic drinks. The family screams, yells, begs, pleads, prays, threatens, or uses the silent treatment. It is all to no avail. So what are kith and kin to do?

Even though families cannot make the alcoholic seek help or stop drinking, they can still be a contributing factor to the alcoholic's gaining sobriety. Even though they cannot do for the alcoholic what that person must do alone, they can hook themselves into a treatment program. They can became aware of the things they should not do. They can learn what they can do to keep the family from total collapse. To an emotionally distraught family, positive guidance can be immensely helpful.

So don't start with the alcoholic member of your family. Start with yourself. Seek out all the resources within the community that will help you to understand the problems you face. Learn the facts that can work in your life and begin to practice them. The family members' most effective tool in helping an alcoholic is the ability to change their attitudes toward the needs of others and to the environment in which they find themselves.

Let us see how the changes made in family members' lives can transform troubled families.

Even though relatives may complain mightily about a family member who drinks too much, they may not understand that they are living with a person who is truly sick. Once you gain knowledge of alcoholism as an illness, the painful situation in which you are living will be far more bearable.

I remember one wife who told me, "I thought my husband was lying to me when he claimed he did not remember choking me. He claimed I put those marks on my own neck, just to accuse him of strangling me. I couldn't believe that he thought I was making up such a story."

This wife could have been spared much emotional trauma if she had known that an alcoholic can suffer a loss of memory, called an alcoholic blackout, without a loss of consciousness.

The family may be relieved to understand that the typical alcoholic behavior is dishonesty, an obnoxious way of finding fault always with others, of never accepting the blame for anything, of never doing anything right. Such behavior is an attempt by alcoholics to cope with their own poor image. It is brought about by their own feelings of fear about themselves, not by the family.

Just understanding that the illness from which your loved one suffers is one that can't be cured—but may be treated and arrested—may give you a whole new lease on life.

Let us look at the typical pattern of interaction within a family that includes an alcoholic; let's also see what happens when the family members find help for themselves.

As the drinking problem worsens, the spouse and children begin to isolate themselves from the extended family in the community. The family drops out of the church and the community and begins to feel social isolation. Tensions make the husband-wife relationship begin to deteriorate. Family members begin to lose self-confidence. No longer do they trust one another.

Children begin to spend the night with friends as often as they can or study late at the library, using any excuse to be absent from the home. No longer do they bring their friends to the house for fear of what will happen. At this point, the

entire family begins to be sick. They feel sorry for themselves. They feel afraid, disgusted, disillusioned. They are
unable to cope with the problems, and the nights become
long and the days dreadful.

As the drinking continues, family members no longer attempt to control the alcoholic. Their main goal is simply to
try to survive on their own. By this time the alcoholic will
have made them feel that they are to blame for everything
bad that happens. They wonder if they have any sanity at
all.

It is at this point that the family desperately needs to
realize that the problems are not their fault. Neither are
they the fault of the alcoholic. Their loved one has simply
developed the illness of alcoholism. No one should feel
guilty. Yet decision making becomes very difficult at this
stage. What should be done? What is right? Who is responsible? The family does not know.

Above all, the family feels the need to protect the alcoholic, to cover up the problems so that others will not
know about them. And as the illness continues, financial
worries are added. The alcoholic loses jobs, writes bad
checks, and is unable to meet the bills. Eventually other
family members take over the making and handling of
money. They dole out to the alcoholic whatever (and however little) they can.

Now the children turn to the nonalcoholic alone to help
them with the decisions in their lives. And the nonalcoholic
uses the children to satisfy emotional needs. The alcoholic
becomes more isolated from the family and feels more rejected and unloved. The family becomes reorganized, with
the alcoholic excluded as much as possible. If the alcoholic
cannot find sobriety, the family may separate at this point.

When the family does continue as a unit, the members
tend to adjust in one of two opposite ways. Either they hide
away, keeping the outside world of community, school, and

church from entering; or they start to run, frantically trying
to stay busy and forget.

You must always remember that the survival of the family does not depend on the alcoholic's getting sober. As long
as you feel that your life depends on the sobriety of the
alcoholic, then the drinking person will always be able to
manipulate you, control you, and misdirect you. This does
not mean to say that you do not want the alcoholic to sober
up and get well.

Howard J. Clinebell, Jr., in a pamphlet entitled "Pastoral
Care of the Alcoholic's Family Before Sobriety," says,
"The most salutary thing that the wife of a drinking al-
coholic can do is to release him. I recall a member of Al-
Anon saying, 'When I got out of the driver's seat, it took a
terrific load off of me.' "

This woman told him that the determination to get her
husband sober had become a passion into which she had
poured herself. The more she failed, the more obsessively
she tried. Somehow her sense of worth as a person had
become bound to her husband's sobriety. He sensed this
fact, and it gave him tremendous power over her.

Finally, after years of futile struggle, she gave up, accepting the fact that nothing she could do would make her husband get sober. In a real sense she had bottomed and sur-
rendered. For the first time in years, she felt a sense of inner
serenity. There's a remarkable parallelism between this
kind of experience and that which the alcoholic must
undergo.

Clinebell continues:

> This surrender invariably produces beneficial results
> in the lives of the wives and children. Frequently it pro-
> duces a positive turning point in the alcoholic's open-
> ness to help. Releasing him means letting go of him emo-
> tionally, giving up all attempts to either control his drink-
> ing or protect him from its consequences.

The wife is able to release him because she has had a surrender experience. She has, in effect, cut the power which he had over her, by no longer needing or attempting to control him.

The alcoholic is often shocked in the change in his wife's response to his behavior. By interrupting the inter-dependency pattern of their relationship, the wife's surrender has produced a crisis in his psychic economy. Her surrender thus may hasten and facilitate his surrender.

He goes on to say, "Releasing the alcoholic frees the wife and children to develop their own potentialities for living."

How wonderful it is when families of an alcoholic recognize that they cannot control their relative's drinking. Assured by the knowledge that they cannot be held responsible for the alcoholic's recovery, they realize that a direct attack on the drinking is futile. They then can abandon this hopeless activity and spend their energies redirecting their own lives.

Sick alcoholics are specialists at arousing family members' anger as well as their anxiety and protective instincts. The alcoholic needs to change. But if the family is to help, they must change too. They must be willing to allow the alcoholic to drink and experience the consequences alone.

Proof of the fact that families do help through surrendering their anxieties are the words I have heard expressed so many times by reformed alcoholics.

"I could never have made it without my family," they tell me. "If they had not stayed by me, I would have gone down in the gutter. The way they really helped me was not by doing it for me but trying to understand my problem. When they understood, I knew they were trying. It really gave me support.

"I didn't need them to tell me what I was doing wrong. I

didn't need them to tell me I was a sorry father and husband. I didn't need all the lectures on alcoholism. I didn't need someone to play the part of God. All I needed was someone to understand me.''

But once the alcoholic does gain sobriety, will the family once again accept him as a member? If the father has been the alcoholic, the wife may have difficulty relinquishing the responsibility and authority which she had to assume while her husband was drinking. She may have had to support the family, make all the decisions, and function both as mother and father. She may find she enjoys possessing such authority. She dislikes returning any of it to her husband now that his drinking is over.

Besides, in the light of his good intentions and broken promises of the past, she may be afraid to trust him. How can she believe in him enough to let him manage the money? Will he continue to have to prove himself?

The rest of the family has similar problems. Will the children once again give him love, accepting him as the father? Will they include him in the family's inner circle? Such trust is very important.

Often members of the family "need" an alcoholic to satisfy their own neuroses or illnesses. Some families like to dominate and control other persons. Alcoholics often become victims of such control. Even after they sober up, the family does not want to lose its dominance. After sobriety has been experienced by the alcoholic, the problems of the nonalcoholic members of the family may be seen to be more serious.

Many times family members neglect to take action for a troubled loved one because they do not know whether or not their relative is actually an alcoholic.

One wife said to me, "Sometimes I'm convinced that my husband is an alcoholic, and other times I'm sure that he is not. He can stay sober for a long time."

You don't determine whether people are alcoholics by how often they drink, what they drink, when or where they drink. Do they take only beer or wine? Do they stay off alcohol for a long time, then go off on a binge? It does not matter. The thing that determines whether they are in trouble with alcohol is what happens to them when they take that drink.

If you are not sure whether you have the problem of alcoholism within your family, it would be well for you to answer a list of test questions, being as truthful as you can. One of the best sets of test questions was given to me by a man who came to me for help. He had found them stuffed in the seat pocket of an airplane, where someone else had left them.

He said, "When I began to take the test, it suddenly dawned on me that my wife had a drinking problem."

I would like to share that list of questions with you. Since there was no identifying organization or author, I cannot give credit, except to say: Thanks to you, whoever you are, for a job well done.

Here they are:

1. Do you worry about your spouse's drinking?

2. Have you ever been embarrassed by your spouse's drinking?

3. Are holidays more of a nightmare than a celebration because of your spouse's drinking behavior?

4. Are most of your spouse's friends heavy drinkers?

5. Does your spouse often promise to quit drinking—without success?

6. Does your spouse's drinking make the atmosphere in the home tense and anxious?

7. Does your spouse deny a drinking problem because your spouse drinks only beer?

8. Do you find it necessary to lie to employer, relatives, or friends in order to hide your spouse's drinking?

9. Has your spouse ever failed to remember what occurred during a drinking period?

10. Does your spouse avoid conversation pertaining to alcohol or problem drinking?

11. Does your spouse justify his or her drinking problem?

12. Does your spouse avoid social situations where alcoholic beverages will *not* be served?

13. Do you ever feel guilty about your spouse's drinking?

14. Has your spouse driven a vehicle while under the influence of alcohol?

15. Are your children afraid of your spouse while he or she is drinking?

16. Are you afraid of physical or verbal abuse when your spouse is drinking?

17. Has another person mentioned your spouse's unusual drinking behavior?

18. Do you fear riding with your spouse when he or she is drinking?

19. Does your spouse have periods of remorse after a drinking occasion and apologize for behavior?

20. Does drinking less alcohol bring about the same effects in your spouse as in the past required more?

If you have answered *yes* to any two of the questions, there is a definite warning that a drinking problem may exist in your family. If you answered *yes* to any four, the chances are that a drinking problem does exist in your family. If you have answered *yes* to five or more, there very definitely is a drinking problem.

Joseph I. Kellermann, director of the Charlotte Council

on Alcoholism, Inc., in his "A Guide for the Family of the Alcoholic," says: "Begin with self. The place to begin in helping an alcoholic's recovery is with self. Learn all you can. Put it into practice, not just into words. This is far more effective than anything you can attempt to do for the alcoholic."

In summation, he lists several rules of thumb to be observed:

1. Learn all the facts and put them to work in your own life. Don't start with the alcoholic.

2. Attend AA meetings, Al-Anon meetings [I would like to add, also, Alateen] and if possible, go to a mental-health clinic, alcoholism information center or to a competent counselor or minister who has experience in this field.

3. Remember you are emotionally involved. Changing your attitude and approach to the problem can speed up recovery.

4. Encourage all beneficial activities of the alcoholic and cooperate in making them possible.

5. Learn that love cannot exist without compassion, discipline and justice, and to accept it or to give it without these qualities, is to destroy it eventually.

It is easier to find a list of *don'ts* in dealing with alcoholics, for it is simpler to understand why you fail than to know how to succeed. The following list, distributed by the Oklahoma City Council on Alcoholism, is not all-inclusive, but it makes a good beginning:

1. Don't allow the alcoholic to lie to you and accept it for the truth, for in so doing, you encourage this process. The truth is often painful, but get at it.

2. Don't let the alcoholic outsmart you, for this

teaches him to avoid responsibility and loses respect for you at the same time.

3. Don't let the alcoholic exploit you or take advantage of you, for in so doing, you become an accomplice in the evasion of responsibility.

4. Don't lecture, moralize, scold, praise, blame, threaten, argue when drunk or sober, pour out liquor, lose your temper or cover up the consequences of drinking. You may feel better, but the situation will be worse.

5. Don't accept promises, for this is just a method of postponing pain. In the same way, don't keep switching agreements. When an agreement is made, stick to it.

6. Don't lose your temper and thereby destroy yourself and any possibility of help.

7. Don't allow your anxiety to compel you to do what the alcoholic must do for himself.

8. Don't try to follow this as a rule book. It is simply a guide to be used with intelligence and evaluation. If at all possible, seek good professional help. You will need it as well as the alcoholic.

9. Above all, don't put off facing the reality that alcoholism is a progressive illness that gets increasingly worse as drinking continues. Start now to learn to understand and to plan for recovery. To do nothing is the worst choice you can make.

Of the many resources within the community to which families of alcoholics may turn, AA, Al-Anon, and Alateen are the best for immediate attention. Many communities also have councils on alcoholism. These referral centers aid the family in researching decisions concerning the need for treatment for the alcoholic. Most specialize in referring those with drinking problems to appropriate sources of therapy, such as the church, counseling centers, and other trained and qualified personnel whose specialty is the alcohol problem.

The council centers are equipped to help alcoholics and their families deal with the particular situation in which they find themselves.

The families may find that as alcoholics become motivated to find assistance they are far more difficult to live with than when the actual drinking was going on.

As one daughter said to me, "Dad's not at home nearly as much now as while he was drinking. After he joined AA he got so wrapped up in all its activities that he has neglected the family even more than he did before."

To overcome this problem, the family can accompany the alcoholic to AA's open meetings. They can participate, themselves, in the Al-Anon or Alateen groups. These activities may help them to accept the fact that the alcoholic's absorption in AA is necessary for recovery, and that eventually a balance will be achieved in the family's routine.

It has been said that "no man is an island." The extent to which an alcoholic will change attitudes and performance will depend in part on the corresponding alterations made in the lives of those who are close to him. The support of the family and the extended family within the community are both necessary.

One of the best ways of preventing future alcoholism is by helping the children of alcoholics. And the best way to aid these youngsters is by restoring the alcoholic parents themselves.

The family that realizes that it needs help personally as much as the alcoholic is often the key that unlocks possibilities of a new and sober life for the alcoholic.

8

Helping Without Hurting

Betty came to my office because she wanted to help her friend. She had known Virginia for years. The two had shared happy times as well as problems. It used to be that Virginia was always on Betty's doorstep if there was trouble. She had been a fun person to be around too.

Now, however, Virginia seemed unable to respond as a friend anymore. The relationship that once ran bubbling and clear as a mountain stream was now polluted by alcohol.

"I've really tried to help Virginia," Betty said. "I've talked to her very frankly about what alcohol is doing to her. I've tried to do it in a sympathetic, loving way. But my talks always end up a disaster." Then Betty looked ashamed. She stared out the window.

"What really bothers me," she almost whispered, "is that now I find my own attitude changing. I guess you might say I'm bitter and resentful. Every time I go out of my way to help Virginia, she just lashes out at me. We always end up arguing and fussing. Heaven help us, we even scream at each other sometimes." Then she looked straight at me.

"Reverend Shipp, I know our fights don't do anything to solve Virginia's problem. I really want to help her, not hurt her. Is there anything I can do to reach out to her that won't make matters worse? And if so, is there any way I can help without getting hurt myself?" I couldn't help sighing.

"Those are questions I've heard so many times before!" I said. "If you are a sensitive, thoughtful person, you soon learn that it is not easy to help alcoholics without hurting them—or getting hurt yourself."

Nor is it a simple task to have compassion for people whose behavior is irritating, whose failure is complete, whose sense of responsibility is lacking, whose manners are repulsive, and whose motivation is weak. A judgmental, unloving, fault-finding, and rejecting person simply cannot help alcoholics.

But many friends, family members, and even other professional helpers who are hurt by an alcoholic's scapegoating, eventually lose sight of their initial desire to help. They can only ask themselves, *Why should I put myself out for someone who is so ungrateful?* This is the point at which Betty seemed to find herself.

"But you still care about Virginia, don't you?" I asked.

"Oh, yes," Betty said. "When Virginia's not drinking, she's the greatest friend I have ever had. But it just doesn't seem to do a bit of good to tell her she's drinking herself to death. Virginia shouldn't have allowed herself to get into this mess. It looks to me as if she's just—well, a sinner. At the very best, I would say she's weak willed."

"Yes, alcoholics can be the most self-centered, demanding, destructive, and cruel people on earth," I agreed. "When they fail, they blame you—the very person who is trying to be of help. You end up getting your heart cut out. You know, Betty, it sometimes seems a miracle that others do care for alcoholics, even when they see them in their ugly moods."

"That's another thing," Betty said. "I'm not an alcoholic myself. Is it really possible for just a plain, ordinary person to help an alcoholic?"

"Yes, it is," I said. "No doubt recovered alcoholics can help others simply because they can identify with their own pain and suffering in the anguish of the person who is still drinking. But you don't have to suffer from a drinking problem yourself to have love and compassion for someone in trouble with alcohol. If you care about people, the nature of their problem will be unimportant—except for how you deal with it."

"But that's my trouble," cut in Betty. "I don't seem to know how to deal with it. I'm really getting hurt very badly."

"There *are* certain things you can do to reduce the risk involved," I said. "But you have to be willing to pay the price to gain the understanding and compassion which are necessary in working effectively with alcoholics." Betty thought about that for a moment. I could almost read her thoughts. She was thinking of the person Virginia could be, and the person she was now.

"I think I'm willing to take the risk," Betty said. "Tell me what I can do."

Perhaps you, too—as a friend, pastor, doctor, social worker, counselor, or just a fellow employee—also want to help someone who is in trouble with alcohol, and you are willing to take that risk. If you do take it, the benefits that you receive will be equal to those gained by the alcoholic. You will find your own life strengthened, your faith deepened, and your hope renewed.

So what is the first step? It is simply to put yourself into the alcoholic's shoes and see the world as he does. You must give up the stereotype which most of us unconsciously have that the alcoholic is "no good," "weak willed," or "only a sinner." You must erase the thought from your mind that alcoholics can change if only they have the desire to do so.

When I was very young, I thought a desert was barren because of a lack of fertility in the soil itself. But later on, when I lived on the desert, it didn't take me long to discover that the soil was far from barren. The real reason nothing can grow is that the blowing sands destroy life. These drifts leave no opportunity for vegetation to grow. When you set up barriers to hold back the drifts, you see new life begin to take hold as if by magic.

By the same token, an alcoholic like Virginia does not have a barren and unfruitful life because she is no good as a person, but rather because of the pattern in which her life has drifted. We find that the first assistance that we can give the alcoholic is to set up barriers that will help stop the drift of a life that appears to be worthless and sterile.

Before alcoholics will let anyone help them put up these barriers, however, they must have confidence and trust in the person who wishes to aid them. Just because we are friends, ministers, doctors, or counselors does not mean automatic acceptance by the alcoholic. We must learn to avoid the mistakes that so many others have made by getting rid of our false impressions.

We need to remember that alcoholics are human beings. They come from every walk of life, every profession and trade, every economic level, every social rank. They may be brilliant or stupid, well educated or unschooled, healthy or sickly, wise or foolish. They may be religious or non-religious. They may be young or old, rich or poor. But they are human beings—children of God.

Yet to these troubled people, alcohol is more significant than self-respect. A bottle rates more than the need or welfare of others. Drinking is more valuable than jobs or standing in the community. To the alcoholic, God is alcohol. Alcohol spells life. To be without it is to die, because in fear, fatigue, and disgust, in physical and emotional pain, the alcoholic needs the service which alcohol renders.

More than anything else, we need to understand the many fears of alcoholics. They are afraid of doing without alcohol—afraid of being called an alcoholic. They fear being hospitalized and facing others after they are sober. The list of fears is endless.

There is no experience in life more frightening to alcoholics than to be without alcohol. It is a fear based on experience. How painful are the remembrances of the shakes, the sweats, the hallucinations, the delirium tremens, the physical and mental anguish. These hurts are etched so vividly in their minds that they can never forget them. The mountain of sobriety rears up so high and seems so painful to climb that the alcoholic does not even attempt to see what is on the other side. If you are going to be helpful to the alcoholic, you have to understand this experience. You must do all in your power to reduce the horror of becoming sober.

Alcoholics also fear the stigma attached to the label "alcoholic." Their major battle in life is to prove that they are not alcoholics. So they must find other excuses for their behavior. They rationalize their drinking both to bolster their own self-esteem and to stave off the social pressures which come at them from all sides.

For this reason it is very important to view alcoholism as an illness. Such a concept enables persons who are drinking too much to begin to accept their alcoholism at the same time that they strengthen their lagging self-respect. They do not have to look into the mirror and see a weakling. Instead they recognize a human being who is suffering from an illness and may be allowed to accept help.

Hanging over the head of many an alcoholic is the sharp-bladed fear of being hospitalized or placed in jail. But there really is no need to fear hospitals anymore, especially if you select the right one. Great advancements have been made in treatment. When you take the time to find out exactly what the treatment is in a specific institution, you may be able to relieve these fears easily.

This is the time when understanding persons are needed,

because they can help the alcoholic accept treatment. However, acceptance will be gained not through fear or being made to feel inferior or wicked, but by a gentle, persuasive spirit expressed in kindness and understanding.

After they have sobered up, alçoholics have another fear. Now they must go back home, face the children, pick up relations with fellow workers, and solve financial difficulties. "Everything just seems so difficult. It's a fearful thing to face," said one man who was ready to return from the hospital.

These, then, are the fears that hang over alcoholics. These are some of the feelings that often make alcoholics seem like two different personalities—one sober and one inebriated.

When alcoholics are sensitive persons, or if they have any pride left, they may even resort to paranoia. "I can't help but drink, because everyone's picking on me," they seem to say. Or they may adopt grandiose behavior to preserve their self-esteem and deny the fact that they are alcoholics.

Actually alcoholics have a very low self-esteem. You can understand this character trait when you view their record of failure in many areas of life, especially in their relationships with other persons. Because they look in the mirror and see a weakling, they feel compelled to rush out and overcompensate in self-reliance.

"Look, Ma, I did it myself," is their rallying cry, but they are unrealistic. They must do absolutely everything on their own without any help. If they can't do it without aid, then they feel they are truly inadequate.

And so they may try to prove the power of their will simply as a means of reinforcing their ego. They may abruptly go on the water wagon, or they may change their drinking patterns. For instance, they may confine their drinking to the happy time at the local bar or to parties where it is acceptable to drink. They may change from "dangerous" whiskey to "innocent" beer or wine.

You see, alcoholics are used to being called all kinds of names. To have to bear the sentence of "alcoholic" is more than they can stand. Be sure the alcoholics that you want to befriend know that you aren't going to put a name to their illness. Let them call it any name they like. It really doesn't matter. What *does* matter is that you help them to see that their pain and their troubles are directly connected with their drinking, regardless of what you call it.

Betty described her friend's Dr. Jekyll and Mr. Hyde personalities this way. "When Virginia is drinking, she is very immature. Her personality seems uncontrollable. She is no longer interested in anyone else. She's very egocentric, thinking only about herself. She seems almost afraid of other people. She isolates herself. She's very dishonest too."

How typical this is of so many alcoholics, I thought. But then Betty went on.

"When Virginia's not drinking, she's an entirely different person. In fact she seems very mature. If anything, she is overcontrolled, overinhibited, extremely honest. She would not think of lying. She's overly considerate of others, always doing more than her share."

I hoped Betty would come to realize she needed to help Virginia see that her problem was not that she was bad but that she was frequently good, perhaps too good for her own benefit. She could best accomplish this task by trying to understand how Virginia felt.

Most alcoholics have four character traits that keep them frustrated, in pain, moody, and desocialized. It is a good idea to take a hard look at these traits.

    1. Alcoholics are frustrated persons because more than likely life has placed them in a situation they do

not like. They drink because alcohol puts everything right. It removes the frustration and makes everything that is terrible about their lives become beautiful.

Alcoholics see a marked discrepancy between the dreams for their future and their actual accomplishments. They are perpetually daydreaming, in a way that is more normal for an adolescent than an adult. They have an immature response to life.

2. Alcoholics are always in pain. Poor physical condition, mental and spiritual problems all cause them to suffer. They are dogged by guilt. Remorsefully, they view the mess they have made of their lives. Whenever they think of themselves, self-pity overwhelms them. Then they feel more and more inferior.

3. Alcoholics are very moody persons. Today they're high; they're the life of the party; everything looks up. Tomorrow they're low, full of self-pity, and sure that the world is at an end. When not under the influence of alcohol, they are extremely self-conscious. Everything that is said, everything that happens, seems to apply to them.

It is impossible for alcoholics to look at themselves and laugh. The way they take themselves so seriously is characteristic of their immaturity. They have an overmastering ego. Either alcoholics play the major role as the star, or they will not be a part of any of life's dramas at all.

4. Most alcoholics are desocialized persons who don't seem to belong. They may pull themselves away from everyone, or paradoxically, they may enjoy being with others. In fact they can be the life of the party. But all are desocialized in this way: They do not derive a feeling of security by belonging to a group or by associating themselves with any institution.

It is not easy to help alcoholics without getting hurt. Nor is it easy to help them without hurting them. You must understand an alcoholic's fears and feelings. You must also have a big heart, an open mind, and a loving spirit.

Unless you love, unless you care, there is no way that you can help another. Anyone who wants to try should turn to the thirteenth chapter of First Corinthians and read it very carefully.

"Love is patient and kind . . ." (v. 4). What patience is required in helping alcoholics—in adjusting our pace to theirs, in answering without irritation the repetitious questions they ask, in patching up their broken lives and hearts.

Think what patience and kindness it takes when alcoholics allow themselves to descend into a self-centered, self-pitying attitude. Their wasted talents and tortured lives remind us of the scattered debris of a wrecked airplane. Once a sleek beauty in the sky, it no longer has power for anything. When healthy persons try to help the sick, they need the grace of God to keep them patient, kind, and understanding.

". . . love is not jealous or boastful" (v. 4). It takes divine grace to keep pride, possessiveness, and domination out of love. It is normal for us to want both to get and to give in love. But if you are going to be helpful, your desire to give must be greater than your desire to get. Helpfulness was never achieved in arrogance or rudeness (*see* v. 5). If we have the kind of love that is wholesome and fine, it will make us sensitive to the persons we are trying to help. We will be considerate of their illness.

I remember one evening I was helping Estelle, one of my church members, as she attempted to bring her husband, Ray, home after he had spent several weeks in a drinking bout. When we drove up to the house, not only the children were waiting. Estelle's mother and father were there. Some of the neighbors were standing around.

As I steadied Ray's trembling arm, I became suddenly very conscious of the reek of alcohol that surrounded us. Ray's clothes were wrinkled, his unshaven face was a prickly cactus. As he fell weakly into a chair, Estelle turned on him and fumed, "There, just take a look at him. There he is, drunk as always—just a no good!"

Then I visited with the group for a while. We talked about Ray's feelings and fears. Finally Estelle put her arms around him, smelly clothing, stubby beard, tearful eyes, and all. "I'm sorry, I didn't know you couldn't help it," she said.

". . . Love does not insist on its own way . . ." (v. 5). We can become so narrow, so self-centered in our own lives that we hinder any kind of treatment for all types of healing.

"Love . . . is not irritable or resentful . . ." (v. 5). If you are going to work with the alcoholic, it is awfully hard not to become hostile and irritable. One of the alcoholic's superweapons is to protect himself or herself by making others angry. If we are going to relate to those who need our help, we must be lifted above our tempers, our angers, our hostilities.

"It [love] does not rejoice at wrong, but rejoices in the right" (v. 6). Resentment runs deeper than irritability or anger. Love is never glad when others go wrong but is eager to believe the best.

"Love bears all things, believes all things, hopes all things, endures all things" (v. 7). Yes, "Love never ends . . . . So faith, hope, love abide, these three; but the greatest of these is love" (vv. 8, 13).

If you are not to run into what one of my friends calls "passion's fatigue" in working with alcoholics, you need faith, hope, and love. You need faith to give you the motivation to work. You need hope for endurance. But you need love to give you purpose, meaning, and heart.

9

Fishers of Alcoholics

> Jesus was walking by the Sea of Galilee when he saw
> two brothers, Simon called Peter and his brother An-
> drew, casting a net into the lake; for they were fisher-
> men. Jesus said to them, 'Come with me, and I will make
> you fishers of men.' And at once they left their nets and
> followed him.
>
> Matthew 4:18–20 NEB

For weeks my young friend Bobby, a city boy, had been
begging his grandfather, Jack, to teach him how to fish.
When, at last, summer came, the two carried their bamboo
poles and bucket of minnows to the banks of a Texas river
shaded by tall, native pecan trees.

At first the nine-year-old enjoyed holding his pole and
watching the water flow over an old dam that once had
served the abandoned mill across the river. But soon he was
bouncing noisily around on the bank, bobbing his pole in
and out of the river. After Jack had to restrain him from
bouncing pebbles across the water, he decided to lay down
the law.

"I thought," said Jack, putting his sunburned hands on
his hips, "that you told me you wanted to learn to fish."

"I do, Grandpa," Bobby said.

"Well, if you do, the first thing you must learn is to love it
enough to do all the things that are necessary. If you don't
love it, we might just as well stay at home," he said.

92

The same can be said of those who would be "fishers" of alcoholics. If you do not like people, if you do not have a deep-seated love for them, the time you spend trying to help them will become nothing but misery. At the same time you will hurt the very ones you are trying to help.

Alcoholics are an especially sensitive kind of "fish." They can tell by the very quiver of your line if you are only kidding about wanting to work with them. If you have all the technical knowledge in the world about helping alcoholics and do not have love, your fishing will be just about as effectual as if you were casting while on water skis, roaring along behind a motorboat.

"Oh, but I *do* love fishing," insisted Bobby. "It's just that I don't believe there are any old fish out there."

"There are more fish out there than you can imagine," Jack said. "But if you want to catch them, you have to learn as much about the water and the fish as you can. You can learn it the hard way—by yourself—or you can listen to your old granddad and others who already know how."

People who want to help alcoholics have the same choice. They can learn by their own painful experiences, or they can accept the guidance of others who are experts already. Bobby quickly saw the point.

"I want you to tell me, Grandpa," Bobby said. His grandfather waited just a moment to make sure the boy was listening.

"Remember," said Jack, "that the river we see flowing over the dam is not the river that the fish see. In our world we can see these pecan trees, the old mill, the slopes coming down to the river. Underneath the surface of the water, the fish can see a landscape just like that. But it is invisible to our eyes."

The life of an alcoholic is the same. Outwardly it may flow along like the placid river waters. Beneath the surface, however, the alcoholic's emotions may be tumbling over a lot of jagged, rusty, metal junk that has been dumped there.

If you are to help alcoholics, you must first see the world as they see it.

"Next," continued my friend Jack, "you must have the right kind of equipment to catch the fish, and you must use it the right way. One reason you have not caught anything is that you are bouncing the pole around too much. And if we didn't have the right kind of line and cork, we would never be able to catch one, either."

You too, to be a fisher of alcoholics, must have the right kind of equipment. You need a sound understanding of alcoholism; you need love and concern for other persons; and you must be able to use your equipment properly if you are to bring your catch safely to shore.

"One very important thing to remember," Jack continued, looking the boy in the eye, "is that to be successful as a fisherman you must be willing to sacrifice to succeed. That means you have to get up early rather than lying in bed till ten A.M. You have to sit quietly on the bank and pay attention. And you can't go skipping those rocks into the river every time you want to."

How much more you must sacrifice if you want to work successfully with alcoholics! Almost everything about helping an alcoholic is inconvenient. When a call for assistance comes, most likely it will come in the middle of the night or at the very time when you had planned something more pleasant to do. Unless you are willing to sacrifice yourself, don't try to go fishing for alcoholics.

One night I fell into bed after a fatiguing day, only to have my telephone ring at 3:00 A.M.

"This is Mac," came the slurred voice of a man I had been trying to help to sobriety. "What you doing?" I could barely keep myself from shouting back at him, "I'm sleeping. What else would I be doing at three A.M.?"

Instead I thought about it from Mac's point of view. As hard as he had tried to stay sober, he'd been drinking. He was hoping I could help.

"It's good to hear your voice," I told him. "I was just waiting for you to call."

But Jack had a lot of other rules to tell Bobby about how to be a good fisherman. "Of course, one of the most important things to remember is that the fish don't come to you," he said. "You can stick a pole in the riverbank and go off and leave it, but if you catch a fish that way it is strictly by accident."

Hardly ever will an alcoholic seek you out for help. It is sad but true that many alcoholics are just waiting for others to make the first move. For many alcoholics the offer is never made.

"And you must above all else have patience. You've got to try and try again," Jack said. "Some people are only too ready to pick up their gear and leave if they don't get a nibble in a hurry. But the fishermen who end up with a good string of fish are the ones who never give up. They are willing to sit by the bank all day if need be. And if that doesn't work, they don't mind coming back another day when the fish are biting."

Sometimes people who work with alcoholics don't make a single catch either. A certain percentage of alcoholics are just not going to respond to anything you do. Yet you must not become discouraged. If you do, your negative feelings will easily damage those whom you are trying to help.

"Once you get a nibble, you can't start pulling your fish in right away," went on Jack. "When you see the cork move a little, give the fish time enough to bite down on the bait. Then jerk the line just right, so you can hook him good. If you jerk him too soon, you will lose him."

Timing is important with alcoholics too. You must know when to leave them alone, when to talk to them, when to be quiet and overlook things. Sometimes you may have to let them go out and do things which seem harmful. And there are other times when you just cannot reach them under any circumstances. To try to do so would mean losing them completely.

"A lot of times you have to fish in the hard-to-reach spots, not the comfortable ones like this bank," Jack pointed out when he saw Bobby's attention lagging. And the same is true of helpers of alcoholics. How often we want to spend our time working with the people who like us, those "nice" ones who do things for us and always cooperate. We simply do not have time to spend with those abusive, ungrateful alcoholics who really need our help most. We're like the housewife who wonders why her house looks dingy and unkempt but keeps on baking cakes instead of using the vacuum cleaner.

But now Jack was concluding his fishing lesson. "If you want to be a good fisherman, you will not always use the same kinds of bait. Some fish go for minnows, some for worms. If you want to catch a gar, you put a hairnet around the bait so that he will get his teeth tangled in it. You have to use just the right kind of bait to attract the fish you are trying to catch."

The same advice goes for fishers of alcoholics. What works with one person who is in trouble with alcohol will turn off another. Even though you may use the same general plan, there are all sorts of ways you can revise the plays to make them especially attractive to the person you want to help.

Yet even when we do all these things—when we know all about the alcoholic and his troubled waters, when we are persistent, willing to sacrifice, when we watch our timing, constantly revise our plans, and commit ourselves to the pathway of love—we sometimes fail.

I believe we can improve our scores if we remember to practice the three A's—alertness, acceptance, and assistance.

First of all, we must be *alert* to the difficulties involved for alcoholics—physically, psychologically, mentally, and spiritually.

We must practice *acceptance*. But there is a great deal of difference between acceptance of alcoholics as persons and approval of their right to drink. Acceptance is merely starting where alcoholics are now, today, falling off the barstool. We don't help them by pointing out their wrongs and putting a not-OK stamp on them.

> . . . He had taken his seat and was engaged in teaching them when the doctors of the law and the Pharisees brought in a woman caught committing adultery . . . . When they continued to press their question he sat up straight and said, 'That one of you who is faultless shall throw the first stone.' When they heard what he said, one by one they went away . . . . Jesus again sat up and said to the woman, 'Where are they? Has no one condemned you?' She answered, 'No one, sir.' Jesus said, 'Nor do I condemn you . . . .'
>
> John 8:2, 3, 7, 10–11 NEB

Alcoholics don't need anyone to tell them that they are failures; that their futures are grim; that they are losing their friends, their loved ones, and their jobs because of their drinking. If you will read the New Testament, you will see that Jesus never spent His time reminding people of their faults. Instead He opened the door to the glorious possibilities of a new life.

I once knew a little boy who had developed quite a reputation as a bully. Almost every day his teachers stood him in the corner "because you're mean." His classmates all called him a "bad boy." His mother constantly reminded him of how many times he had been sent to the principal's office. His bad conduct, she said, was going to kill her if he didn't change. "You do nothing but misbehave. I wouldn't be surprised if you ended up in jail," she warned him.

One day this boy felt a strong urge to grab a smaller friend's bicycle away from him and ride off on it. Distraught, his mother yelled, "Good little boys don't do things like that! Why can't you ever help younger children instead of hitting them?" But the youngster only hung his head and blurted out, "Because I can't. I'm not a good little boy. You already told me I was bad."

Alcoholics don't need reporters to write headlines about everything they've been doing wrong. They know the story by heart. What they need is a friend who can point not a finger of scorn, but the way to a better life.

But alcoholics don't need to be ignored, either. Some churches have been known to "forget" about the member who has been discovered to be an alcoholic. Even worse, alcoholics are sometimes pushed out of the church and cut off from many church activities. They are made to feel unwelcome. And finally they are lost to the church. Yet you don't build a fire by throwing cold water on the coals. Nor does a coach build a good football team by leaving his players to themselves.

> Entering Jericho he made his way through the city. There was a man there named Zacchaeus; he was superintendent of taxes and very rich. He was eager to see what Jesus looked like; but, being a little man, he could not see him for the crowd. So he ran on ahead and climbed a sycomore-tree in order to see him, for he was to pass that way. When Jesus came to the place, he looked up and said, 'Zacchaeus, be quick and come down; I must come and stay with you today.' He climbed down as fast as he could and welcomed him gladly. At this there was a general murmur of disapproval. 'He has gone in,' they said, 'to be the guest of a sinner.'
>
> Luke 19:1–7 NEB

All the good people called Zacchaeus nothing but a sinner. But Jesus did not call Zacchaeus names; He called him by name. There is a difference. Today the same disapproval too often surrounds the friends, the minister, or helpers who rub elbows with alcoholics in order to help them. Perhaps Jesus already knew Zacchaeus' name because all the others had so busily gossiped about him. But Zacchaeus would never have found a new and joyous life if Jesus had simply listened to this condemnation. Instead He called him by name.

Besides practicing alertness and acceptance, fishers of alcoholics need to remember the third A, which stands for *assistance*. You must not be afraid or reluctant to call for help yourself if you are to help alcoholics. There is a job for the professional therapist and the psychiatrist that they alone can perform. But alcoholics also need you, their teachers, ministers, physicians, and social workers. They need their fellow employees, their club presidents, their church-school teachers, their friends. They need the family, the church, Alcoholics Anonymous, and counseling centers. Seek all kinds of help for the alcoholics you wish to help.

You must have humility enough to realize that no one person can have all the answers to alcoholics' problems, because alcoholics are very complicated people. No one formula, no one person will be able to do everything for the alcoholic. The person you are trying to help is very special. Each case is different.

Helping alcoholics renew their lives is considerably different from building a future from scratch. A couple I knew bought an older home in a good neighborhood, planning to remodel it completely. The tiny, crowded kitchen was a disgrace. It was little more than a hallway. But if a wall could be removed between it and the adjacent breakfast room, the kitchen would have room for all the latest conveniences—a dishwasher, a utility closet, and a pleasant dining area too. But when they called in the architect, they were aghast. The wall that separated the kitchen from the breakfast area was the main support of the second floor. To remove it would be disastrous.

Before you remove the alcohol which has been supporting alcoholics for so long, you must first learn why the drinking way of life became necessary in the first place. If you simply take it away, you may find the whole person tumbling down in ruin. One of the hardest lessons for all helpers, including professionals, to learn is that you must substitute a good foundation for the bad support that alcohol has provided.

Jesus recognized this truth when He said:

> When an unclean spirit comes out of a man it wanders over the deserts seeking a resting-place; and if it finds none, it says, 'I will go back to the home I left.' So it returns and finds the house swept clean, and tidy. Off it goes and collects seven other spirits more wicked than itself, and they all come in and settle down; and in the end the man's plight is worse than before.
>
> Luke 11:24–26 NEB

A wise kindergarten teacher never demands that the little boy who has grabbed another child's toy give it up. She simply finds a more interesting toy to show him, and he will quickly leave the other child alone and seek out the new plaything. But the new toy must have real play value if it is to hold his attention.

Do not take away the drink that has sustained an alcoholic without offering a program of value. As Paul might say, "Put on the new, and the old will fall away" (*see* Ephesians 4:24).

The live-oak tree loses its leaves like all other deciduous trees, yet it always appears green. That is because it holds on to its leaves all winter. In the spring, as new leaves are forming, the old drop away naturally, without ever leaving the tree bare and exposed.

You, then, must support and encourage the alcoholic while he is in the transition period from alcoholism to sobriety. Jesus told us to go the second mile, and we may have to be willing to go even a third or fourth. We might even have to initiate the action ourselves.

In the past I have often asked alcoholics what hour of the night is the roughest for them for, almost always, they awaken in the early predawn hours. Unable to sleep, they must fight the urge to take that first drink. When I learn what their hour of temptation is, I sometimes have set my alarm for that time, wakened, and called by telephone to say, "I know this may be a bad time for you, and I just wanted to let you know you are not alone. I'm pulling for you tonight. I know you can make it."

If you are to be a fisher of alcoholics, you are going to have to love them and go after them. You have to fish or stay at home and cut bait. But loving someone is a lot more involved than just telling him so. We who are Christians can tell alcoholics that God loves them, that Christ died for them, that we love them and are sure that God will make everything right for them when they give up alcohol. But it is not enough to say these things. Somehow alcoholics must learn to know all that for themselves.

Love has two sides—a receiving and a giving element. Persons who only receive love may become weak. It is only when they learn to give love that they build strength for themselves.

Surgeons don't tell their patients to lie in bed to recover their health after an operation. No, their patients are required to get up out of the hospital bed even when it is painful to do so. Only in this way can they regain their health.

Those helpers who try to carry all the alcoholics' burdens for them soon find alcoholics turning away in frustration. Many affluent parents give their children everything that money can buy. They love their children, yet they destroy them. When the children grow up, they sometimes reject their parents because they see them as the persons who have undermined them by giving them everything.

It is not until alcoholics love God through Christ that there will be any change in their drinking way of life. When they are enabled not just to receive love, but to love back, they will become whole.

". . . If any man will come after me, let him deny himself, and take up his cross and follow me" (Matthew 16:24 KJV).

Jesus did not say that He would carry the alcoholics' cross. Instead He said, "For whosoever will save his life shall lose it: and whosoever will lose his life for my sake shall find it" (Matthew 16:25 KJV).

Alcoholics Anonymous has a remarkable record in rehabilitating alcoholics because it undergirds each member with love and understanding. When alcoholics enter AA, they are much in need of receiving love. But AA is not just one step, but twelve. It is only when alcoholics have learned to go out and give away what has been given to them within the organization that they are truly strong. The Twelfth Step is what makes the alcoholic whole.

Once a sick man was carried to Jesus on his bed. First Jesus let the man know that he was loved when He forgave him. But Jesus did not offer to carry the sick man's bed or give him money. Instead He said, "Arise, take up thy bed, and go into thine house" (Matthew 9:6 KJV). When the man did so, the multitudes marveled.

If you can enable alcoholics to carry their own beds, if you can inspire them to love back and give back and walk on their own two feet, you will enable them to find a new life. They will then be able to say gratefully, "The Lord is my shepherd; I shall not want," rather than confess, "Alcohol is my shepherd; I shall want for ever."

Women Need Help Too

My wife and I had just returned home from church services when the Sunday-school-nursery teacher phoned me.

"Oh, Reverend Shipp, I'm afraid something terrible has happened. It's almost one P.M., and everyone's gone home, and Edith Jones still hasn't come for little Jimmy," she said.

"Did Edith say anything about being delayed when she left Jimmy?" I asked.

"No, she just said she was going to Sunday school. But she was acting sort of strange."

"What do you mean?"

"She just looked strange. She was walking unsteadily. What I mean is, it looked as if she'd been drinking."

Edith Jones—drinking? As my wife and I drove back to the church I tried to remember everything I could about the Joneses. They seemed a nice young couple enjoying their first child. Edith hadn't married until she was almost thirty. Although she had been a successful career woman, she was now staying at home to be a full-time mother to Jimmy. The Joneses came to church fairly often. Edith even brought Jimmy to Sunday school when Burt was out of town, as he was this morning. If Edith had a drinking problem, I didn't know about it.

We found Jimmy hungry, cross, and sleepy.

"I want my mommy," was all he seemed able to say. No, he didn't know where Mommy was. When we drove to the

Joneses' house and found no one at home, he seemed to think we were the ones who were keeping her away. We took Jimmy home. While my wife fed him, I began to make phone calls.

We called the Jones house and got no answer. We phoned a number of her friends. No one could say where Edith Jones was. My wife put Jimmy to bed for his nap.

It was almost suppertime before Edith rang our doorbell. She stood there, a petite young woman with dark hair that looked disheveled and eyes that were red-rimmed.

"Do you still have Jimmy here?" she said, speaking slowly with only a touch of slurring. "A friend of mine told me you had him here."

"Yes, Jimmy's here," I said. "Come in."

"I've been looking everywhere for him. I was so worried!" she said.

"But don't you remember? You left him at the church nursery," I said. She looked terribly confused then, and right away I knew what had happened.

"Let's sit down a moment and talk," I said. "I think it would be dangerous for you to try to drive home and take care of Jimmy in your condition."

"What do you mean, my condition?" she said.

"You've been drinking, haven't you?" I asked. She stared at me a moment, and then she started to cry.

"Yes, I have—and I'm so scared. I don't even remember where I was all afternoon. I just woke up and found that Jimmy wasn't in the house. I was so afraid something had happened!"

"That's called a blackout," I said. "Have you ever had one before?"

"No, never," she said, then looked ashamed. "I guess I should be honest. Yes, I have blacked out before, and I have been drinking too much. I know I have. I get so bored and depressed just staying home and keeping house. Burt told me I'd be all right once the baby came, but I haven't gotten better. I've gotten worse, and he won't let me go back to work. What am I going to do?"

"Have you tried to get help for your problem?" She began to cry harder at this question.

"I have wanted to—really. But Burt doesn't want anyone to know I drink; my parents don't either. They just keep telling me I can stop if I try. But, Reverend Shipp, I've tried. I have. And I just can't stop!"

I sighed. I'd heard Edith's story before. When the alcoholic is a woman, her family often tries to hide the problem—and the alcoholic herself—away in a back bedroom. While their loved one dies a little more each day, they "protect" her from a society they know will judge her much more harshly than if she were a man.

Women who are in trouble with alcohol have the same need for support and aid that male alcoholics do. But female alcoholics too often are tolerated with amusement by friends and looked on with contempt by their families. The city in which a female alcoholic lives does not even provide her with a Skid Row where she may retreat as a last resort. Her Skid Row is in a back bedroom where she can be hidden away, rejected, left alone to handle the problem by herself. Hers is a pathetic story.

In fact the world's sympathy usually does not go to the alcoholic wife (even though she is the one in need of it), but to her husband. Her guilt goes on increasing because of this attitude. In reality the man often is encouraging his wife to drink in order that he may receive solicitous attention. People are so busy feeling sorry for the husband that they cannot see how he is contributing to her illness. They are blind to his indifference, his neglect, his terrible treatment of her.

But there are clinics for women who are alcoholics. And surely drinking women realize they need help. Why do the numbers of females in trouble with alcohol increase while the clinics are ignored? Why do women try to solve their problems alone?

Fear of being found out as an alcoholic is perhaps the most important reason. Society tolerates alcoholism among men. A man who drinks too much doesn't raise many eyebrows. But a woman is not expected to have problems or become intoxicated. If she does, she is despised and rejected.

Even the labels which people attach to female drinkers are far more damaging than those describing male alcoholics.

One man called me and said, "I wonder if you could help my wife with her drinking problem." Then he added bitterly, "I guess I shouldn't really call her a wife. She's just a pig. She sits around drinking her slop all day and smells like she's been wallowing around in a mudhole made of sewage. Yes, that's what she is all right—nothing but a pig!"

After his wife had sobered up, she told me it was much harder to forget the cruel things that had been said to her than to recover from the illness itself. She will forever bear the scars of her husband's tongue-lashing. Even today she sometimes wakes after a nightmare with the word *pig* ringing in her ears.

While women have enough foresight to seek help for the male alcoholics in their families, it is remarkable that many refuse to look for assistance for themselves. They are afraid of being exposed. And the family too often keeps the lid of its Pandora's box clamped tightly over her and all their troubles. Their attitude makes it very difficult for her to be motivated to gain sobriety. It does not create an environment conducive to healing.

Besides the fear of being found out, women have some very practical considerations that stand in the way of seeking help. For if she needs to go away for treatment, who will care for the children, cook the meals, keep the clothing in good order? Her absence, she knows, disrupts the family far more than would her husband's.

Other women are afraid to admit their addiction and find assistance because they fear their husbands will seek divorces. And in some cases the fear is based on reality. Most men have trouble facing the illness of a woman. Witness the inability of most men to stay in a hospital room longer than fifteen minutes. They feel the same way about a wife suffering from the illness of alcoholism. They get out of the marriage rather quickly, seeking separation or divorce.

Ironically, most women married to alcoholic husbands usually stick by their mates for a long time, trying to help them overcome their addiction.

Yet I should not make such a blanket statement concerning men. For I have seen husbands who have stood by their wives faithfully, year after year, cooperating in every way to bring about a recovery.

But many men, lacking patience and tolerance, rely on force. The threat of a divorce is the weapon they often use to try to make their wives stop drinking.

Another dominating fear for women is the threat of losing their children. After Ron and Judy had enjoyed a good marriage for twelve years, Judy developed a drinking problem. Ron threatened divorce if she did not stop; then he even swore he would take the children away too. Finally he persuaded her to sign herself into a state hospital for treatment.

"I promise I won't take the children away if you get help," he told her. But while she was undergoing treatment, Ron filed for divorce and asked for custody of the children.

The case went before the jury. Ron had no trouble rounding up witnesses to testify how the children had suffered while Judy drank. Judy, still at a low point emotionally and lacking time or money to pay for good legal aid, made a poor showing. The divorce was granted, with custody awarded to Ron.

Judy was crushed. For a long time everything was downhill for her, though at last, after much help, she was able to turn her life around and gain sobriety.

Perhaps if more child-care services were available when women seek treatment, they would have less fear of admitting their alcoholism and losing their children.

There is little doubt that female alcoholics do have many logical fears about trying to get help. Furthermore they are able to hide their condition much longer than can men, especially if they do not work outside the home. If their husbands travel a lot or work late at night, they have the perfect place in which to drink in private—the home. All they have to do is avoid answering the doorbell and the telephone. No one ever knows.

Men who drink too much usually do not have such privacy. Their wives can't help but witness the problem. Most women then push their husbands to ask for help or seek it themselves.

There is a general belief that women, with their more emotional makeup, are more difficult to treat for alcoholism than men are. Basically there is little difference. Women may develop into alcoholics a bit more rapidly than men. And because women can hide more easily, they are harder to reach. But, on the plus side, women do seem to have a greater tolerance for pain. They have a lot of fight once they make up their minds to get sober. Given the right kind of understanding and a good support system, women have the faith and hope that will make their chances of recovery good.

While alcoholic mothers can hide better, it is virtually impossible to protect the children from the effects of their drinking, as can be done with fathers. Women can usually shield their children from intoxicated fathers. But when the mother is drinking, the children never know what to expect. Her relationship with them, which almost never is one of a mature person, changes daily. She may be in a jolly mood today, a black depression tomorrow, and an angry temper tantrum the day after that.

As one child said to me, "When Mother's drinking, there is no way you can please her. Everything I do is wrong. She accuses me of doing awful things—like lying, cheating, and stealing. You name it, and she claims I have done it."

The woman who is an alcoholic in the home is the seed that sprouts children who are maladjusted and lack confidence. But a woman does not have to be told the importance of her role. She knows it. When she drinks too much and cannot function in this role, she feels she has disgraced herself as well as her family.

A man can go through similar drinking experiences and show little or no remorse—probably because his wife holds the family together for him. When the mother drinks, the family is disrupted. In addition she suffers a deep feeling of shame and guilt.

If you must choose between seeking help and disturbing your family because of it, make sure your choice is to find assistance. The consequences will not be nearly as damaging as having your family unhappy—angry at everything you do. Don't be afraid that you will lose your loved ones. The odds are that if you continue drinking, you will be deprived of them more quickly.

In most cases, if you seek help and gain sobriety, you will keep your family and regain your health, your self-respect, your confidence, and your faith in life.

Sobriety has to be your number-one priority. Even though you may not have the support of your family at the beginning, there is a way out. You have the help of God. And most communities have resources to aid you.

You may feel that when you try to find professional assistance you are simply advertising the fact that you cannot drink. You may fear being labeled an alcoholic or being ridiculed. But remember there is nothing bad that anyone can say or think about those who are strong enough to seek treatment and find a program that will help them stop drinking. There is no way that anything anyone says can be as bad as what they say and think about you while you are drinking.

People who say derogatory things about you for getting sober and staying that way are certainly not your friends. They do not have your interests at heart. Actually such people may have their own problems which are every bit as serious as yours. The only difference may be that theirs is not a drinking problem.

So don't be afraid to look for help, even if you have to do it on your own. You will have demonstrated that you have wisdom and insight enough, strength and courage enough, to face your problem and do something about it.

In a short time your friends will get used to the idea that you don't have to drink, you can't drink, and that you're not going to take a drink.

When Frank and his wife, Martha, came to see me, Frank was very unhappy. Their marriage was about to break up. He felt that something was wrong with Martha, but he did not know what.

After I talked to them a few moments, it was obvious that Martha was either drinking or on drugs. I was almost sure the problem was alcohol.

"Are you willing to look at your drinking problem, Martha?" I asked. At that, Frank's face flushed.

"Do you mean to tell me you're accusing my wife of being an alcoholic?" he demanded.

"No," I said. "But obviously she does have a problem. I just asked if she was willing to look at it."

"Why, Martha has never taken a drink in her life. You can check with her friends if you don't believe me. No one has ever seen her take a drink."

I found out later that what he said was true. No one, not even Martha's husband, had ever seen her drink. She had been hidden.

But now Martha was interrupting. "Frank, stop yelling," she said. "It's true. I've been drinking for six years. In fact I haven't had a sober day for two years. If you want to know how bad my drinking is, just go home and count all the empty bottles under the house." Frank's face seemed to go up in flames.

"But how could you drink so much? Where did you get the money for it?"

Martha hung her head. "I've been using the fifty dollars you set aside each week to give to the church," she admitted. I believe Frank could have accepted almost any other problem more easily than the fact that Martha was drinking. He just sat and fumed.

"Frank, I'm willing to join AA and get sober," she said. But at this he jumped up and almost snarled at her.

"Just let me tell you this, Martha. If you join that bunch of drunks, I'll leave you. I'll ruin you!" Then he stomped out of the room.

Martha and I had a long talk.

"I know I can't get sober alone," she said. "I've tried day after day for the past two years. God only knows how I've tried! I've got to have help, but I don't want to lose my husband."

I asked her to hold steady for a few days. I thought perhaps I could help Frank understand her needs. But Frank refused to talk to me. He quit coming to church and wouldn't speak to Martha.

I asked a wonderful woman who was a member of AA to visit Martha. The day after she did so, Martha joined AA. Together we helped her see that her first priority was to gain sobriety.

"Once you get sober you'll be your old self again. You'll be a good wife and mother, and I am confident Frank will be glad that you joined AA. Just be sure at this particular time that your AA does not interfere with Frank," I told her.

I never saw anyone work at the AA program with greater commitment and determination than Martha. She knew that the AA way meant life or death for herself and her family too.

It wasn't long before things began to change for the better. Suddenly Frank realized he had his true wife back again. He took a one-hundred-and-eighty-degree turn to support what she was doing. He found his way back to the church.

You should hear the compliments he pays his wife now. He can't say enough good things about AA. He has joined the Al-Anon group so that he can better understand the AA program and himself.

There comes a time when you may have to seek help, even though your family may be against it. Only you will know when that has to be done.

Just remember, you do not walk alone. God walks with you.

11

Helping the Youngster Make the Right Decision

It is hard to believe the statistics on the growing number of subteens and teenagers who are already alcoholics or are in trouble with alcohol. Doctor Maurice Shevitz, director of the National Institute on Alcohol Abuse and Alcoholism, in 1975 published the first reports of their kind on the research done by the federal government on the subject of young alcoholics in "Youth and Their Use of Alcohol."

"Approximately 500,000 teen-agers are alcoholics," Doctor Shevitz reported. "Of the young people between the ages of 13 and 24, one out of five are already alcoholics, and another 5% will become alcoholics."

Furthermore this report shows that between seventy-one percent and ninety-two percent of all high-school students drink. Of male senior-high students, fourteen percent get drunk at least once a week, and thirty-six percent at least four times a year. Translated into numbers, 1,130,000 youths between the ages of twelve and seventeen get drunk, not just high, at least once a week.

Even among twelve-year-olds, two percent get drunk once a week. And by the tenth grade, fifty percent of the nation's youth report they are drinking at night and in cars.

Of these findings, Doctor Shevitz said, "It just blows my mind."

Some teenagers and even subteens become alcoholics be-

fore their parents even realize they are drinking. Perhaps
mothers and dads may see a moodiness, a withdrawal, a
sudden drop in school grades, or a general change in personality but write these developments off as part of adoles-
cence.

When Joe was only twelve years old, his mother became
so worried about the changes she saw in him that she called
me.

"He does nothing but stay in his room behind a closed
door that we don't dare open. But I know he's not studying,
because he just got a terrible report card. He used to be a
pretty decent kid. But now he just can't seem to do anything right," she said. "Can you help us?"

"I'll try. Would you like to come in and talk about it?" I
said.

She said she would. Since she seemed very troubled, I set
an appointment as soon as possible. I invited her to bring
her husband and her son too.

When they came into my office, my first impression was
that here was a typical middle-class American family. The
parents were well-groomed, the father in a business suit and
tie, looking a bit pudgy from too many of the good dinners
prepared by his wife, an attractive, well-dressed woman
with a sweet, motherly smile. Joe looked like a typical
twelve-year-old too, his suddenly grown tall body still looking as fragile as a girl's.

Joe took a seat on a chair that was as far away as possible
from the sofa on which his parents sat. He hid his expres-
sion behind the glasses that looked enormous on his slen-
der, freckled face.

While I made small talk to put the family at ease, Joe
kicked at the carpet and twisted in the chair. First he picked
up the ashtray on the nearby table and examined it; then he
put it down. A few seconds later he grabbed it and studied it
again. And all the while he said nothing. I could see that he

was so uptight, nervous, and anxious that he could hardly sit still.

"Joe, would you like to go for a walk? Maybe we can stop for a Coke," I said. He almost jumped up out of his chair.

"I sure would," he said. While we were drinking our Cokes, I put it to him.

"Would you mind talking about your problem in front of your parents?" I asked. Joe looked down at the Coke.

"What problem?" he said.

"Your drinking problem," I said.

"How did you know?" he said.

"Well, Joe, it's very obvious that you've been drinking," I said. He thought about that a moment; then he let out a big sigh.

"I thought no one would ever notice," he said, almost as if he had been clinging to a life raft, waiting to be rescued from a stormy sea. "No, I don't mind talking about it, but you'll have to help. Mom and Dad won't understand. And they'll be mad—awful mad."

The parents were the ones who now looked uptight and anxious when we returned to my office. The father leaped up out of his chair.

"Well, what's wrong with Joe? Is he on drugs? We knew he was acting like a dope head!" he almost shouted. I shook my head.

"No, it's not that," I said. "Joe, would you like to tell them?" Joe hesitated a moment. Then, in a voice so low you could hardly hear it, he said, "Dad, I'm hooked on alcohol."

When Joe's father heard that, the anxiety drained out of his face. His shoulders seemed to relax. He sat back down in the chair.

"Thank goodness!" he said. "I thought it was something bad like dope. If it's just alcohol, we can handle that."

"How do you plan to handle it for your son?" I asked.

"We'll make him stop, that's what we'll do," the father said irritably.

"But I don't think you understand," I said. "What if he can't stop?" The father looked at me as if I were a policeman who had just given him a ticket for going through a yellow light.

"You're not accusing my boy of being a *drunk*, are you?" he demanded. "Who ever heard of a twelve-year-old being an alcoholic?" The more he thought about it, the angrier he got. Suddenly he leaped out of his chair and lunged at me like a boxer, standing over me and shaking his finger in my face.

"We've never even seen Joe drunk. How dare you insinuate that our son is an alcoholic?" he yelled. But now Joe had jumped up and grabbed his father's arm. He was almost crying.

"Dad, don't do that. I've been drunk for a long time. I haven't even had a sober day in six months!"

The father's anger exploded like a popped balloon. Now he was staring at Joe as if he were a stranger. I could well understand his shock. It was hard for me, also, to believe that this innocent-looking boy with the freckles across his nose was an alcoholic.

Joe's mother, still sitting on the sofa, was dabbing at her eyes with a tissue.

"But, Joe, you're not even old enough to buy liquor. How can you possibly be an alcoholic?" she asked.

"But I am, Mom," Joe said. She shook her head.

"But you don't even understand what an alcoholic is," she insisted. Joe then turned to me.

"You know that list of questions that you have in your outer office? Can I bring them in here?"

"Certainly," I said. I knew he was referring to the list of questions that I had prepared for youth who are in trouble with alcohol. I had just "happened" to leave them where Joe would see them when he came in.

Quickly Joe brought the list of questions. It was interesting to see that now he sat down between his mom and dad. Methodically he read them out loud.

Here they are:

1. Would you feel resentful and angry if your parents questioned you about your drinking?

2. Has your drinking affected your schoolwork? Have you missed school as a result of your drinking?

3. Has it affected your relationships with your parents and teachers as well as your peers?

4. Do you find yourself associating only with peers who drink?

5. Do you feel you need to stop drinking in order to get things under control?

6. Have you noticed any change in your ability to do your schoolwork or concentrate on your work?

7. Do you find yourself sitting in class wishing you could have a drink?

8. Do you ever sneak a drink while at school?

9. Would you be uneasy, shaken up, or bored if you found you could not get a drink?

10. Have you ever tried to stop drinking, only to find that you could not?

11. Have your peers ever tried to get you to stop drinking or indicated that you were drinking too much?

12. Do you ever take a drink before you leave for school?

13. Do you drink with others, or would you rather drink alone?

14. Would you feel uneasy about attending a school function or party if there were no alcohol available?

15. Do you drink to get high?

16. Do you drink to get smashed?

17. Do you in selecting your friends find it necessary that they share your interest in drinking?

18. Is your drinking getting worse?

19. Do you frequently feel the need to drink?

20. Does your personality change when you drink?

21. Do you argue, fight, or become angry when you drink?

22. Are there things you would like to do in your life but find that drinking interferes?

After Joe read these questions, he pointed to the footnote which said: "If you answer any seven of these with *yes,* the chances are you're in trouble with alcohol."

"Mom and Dad, I had to answer most of them *yes,*" he said in a low voice.

Thirty-five years ago, when I first started working with people in trouble with alcohol, I found that most of the drinking among young people was done by the men, not the women. Their drinking was usually limited to the latter half of the senior year. When the graduation celebrations were over, the drinking was ended. For yesterday's young people, drinking, like the high-school diploma, was proof of being an adult.

Today the use of alcohol among young people is almost universal. Many teenagers now use alcohol for the same purpose they once used drugs, simply because their parents seem to find alcohol more acceptable.

Joe's parents were relieved when they found their son was not addicted to drugs, but only alcohol. Their attitude indicated their lack of knowledge about the problem that confronted Joe. It is frightening to know that so many youth are dependent on alcohol today. It is probably the number-one drug being used by American youth.

Schoolteachers have told me they have found grade-school pupils coming to school drunk. One mother of an eleven-year-old boy told me she discovered her son carrying alcohol to school in his lunch-box thermos bottle. He wasn't drinking just to "act smart." He was drinking to get high at school.

The father of another young man who was fourteen came to see me along with his son. This father hadn't been able to believe that his son had a drinking problem until the police chased him for fifty miles at speeds up to 105 miles per hour before they finally caught him. The next day the boy could not even remember having been in his car, much less taking part in such a wild chase scene.

How do young people get started drinking? They are taught to do so, many by their parents. The adult world influences their thinking. Many young people receive their first drink in the home.

Youth who have participated in studies on drinking reveal the following reasons for taking the first drink: having a drink offered by the parents; taking a drink during a special celebration or holiday; giving in to the curiosity to see how it tastes, to see what the effects are, to learn if all the stories which they have heard about drinking are true.

The reasons why youth continue to drink are different, according to what they report. Some of them are: to join with the rest of the group; to be sociable; to gain personal enjoyment.

But parents often ask me, "Why does my teenager drink?" This much-asked question has as many answers as there are teenagers who drink. As with adults, youngsters have many reasons for drinking, and some of their reasons are different from those of adult alcoholics.

Social pressure is one factor with which American young people must deal in making the decision as to whether to drink. In the language of adolescents, *being different* translates "being a failure." If their circles of friends drink, it may be very difficult to be the only one who does not. While peer-group pressure is not considered to be as great an influence as it once was, for many youngsters it is still a very real motivation.

But why can some teenagers withstand social pressure while others succumb to it? Sometimes the fault has to be shared by the parents, as well as the peers. Young people all have a need for feeling independent. When teenagers have not been allowed by their parents the needed responsibility for making decisions, they become especially susceptible to group pressure. Their decision to go along with the crowd could well be an act of rebellion against the parents, who did not allow the opportunity for independence and decision making.

Many parents make all the decisions for their children. Then when the children are with a group, they do not feel they are capable of saying *no* to others' suggestions.

Many young people associate drinking with having fun. Like many in the adult world, they cannot think of having a party without booze.

"I haven't been to a party in over a year where there was no alcohol available," fourteen-year-old Dan told me. "If you don't drink, you feel out of place, odd. You're different. Besides, it makes you feel good and puts you in a happy mood. You get a thrill when you drink. I wouldn't think of going to a party without having a few drinks under my belt, and I don't ever plan to stop drinking. If I did, I would stop going to parties."

Much teenage drinking is connected with celebrating the special occasion. On more than one occasion, seventeen-year-old Mary had seen her parents inviting friends to stop by for a drink following a football game. So when her school won the big district football game, she invited her friends to celebrate at her home. Her parents were out of town, and Mary was supposed to be spending the night with friends. But her group always celebrated a football victory with a drinking party.

Mary borrowed freely from the large supply of alcohol in her father's liquor cabinet. In her mind, as well as in the minds of most young people and adults, alcohol is the thing that "makes" the celebration.

But Mary hadn't counted on the effects of alcohol. The celebration quickly got out of hand. Finally she called me. And when I arrived, Mary was hysterical, because the house was a shambles.

Another reason why teens use alcohol is to drink with their friends. While most young people may not feel they have been coerced into drinking by their peers, the fact remains that friends who drink usually drink together. If alcohol plays an important role in the life of your youngsters, you can rest assured that they will seek out friends who also drink.

Young people who don't drink usually have more friends who also do not use alcohol. Abstainers can make a group of drinkers feel so guilty that they are dropped if they don't soon conform.

Some young people use alcohol because they see it as a symbol of adulthood. "You can drink when you become a man," many boys have heard. So drinking becomes the nuts and bolts of building manhood. For many young men, and women, too, drinking appears to be the "smart" thing to do, simply because they see the majority of grown-ups drinking. Besides, the process of achieving true adulthood is a difficult and time-consuming one. Teens sometimes try to take a shortcut to the adult life-styles they have observed by hitting the bottle.

Lest we be too critical of their attempts to attain instant maturity, let us realize that one of the strongest pressures to drink comes from their association with adults whom they admire. Most youngsters will choose their parents as models to follow. For this reason, the parents' drinking patterns influence the child's.

Many young people drink because they are simply bored stiff. They don't know any other way to use their leisure time than the way adults do—which is to drink. Without questioning the values of drinking, they fall into the custom.

Paul's father sent his son from a distant town to visit with me because of a drinking problem. Paul made it clear that the kids in his town were always bored stiff. They didn't have anything wholesome to do.

"I just always seem to mess it up," Paul admitted. "About all we do in the evenings is gather at a place outside town and sit around in a car and drink beer. The next morning I don't feel like getting up and going to school. We end up playing hooky, and then we have more time to kill, so we drink during the day as well as at night."

Some young people drink because they feel they are failures. In their own eyes they just don't measure up to their schoolmates, or they have not fulfilled their parents' expectations. Alcohol contributes to a feeling of self-importance and success.

No doubt some teens drink to escape a hopeless situation within their families or in their own despairing lives. We have seen a generation of young people whose life-style is very destructive because of their lack of feelings of self-worth.

Seldom do youth think of what alcohol does to them, but they often consider what it can do for them. The young person who is physically weak can feel as strong as a weight lifter with a few drinks. A young lady who sees herself as ugly can feel like Miss America. One who is inhibited suddenly becomes free.

One young man expressed it the only way he knew. "Down deep I feel there's something wrong with me. I have these funny feelings—I don't know why," he said. "But after a few drinks they seem to disappear.''

Some young people drink because they are emotionally disturbed. When these people begin to solve their problems and gain their satisfactions in life by the aid of a chemical, they become dependent on it. They are on the road to addiction. Yet the price they have to pay in injured health and degradation does not seem too great to pay.

Youth also drink to bring about the moment of excitement or exaltation that comes when feelings take complete charge of their personality. They are seeking a thrill. While there is a basic need for release of emotional tension, for moments of excitement in life's sameness, there is nothing normal about using the chemical alcohol to achieve it.

But not all young people drink, just as not all adults drink. Again there are many reasons why they do not. Some teenagers don't drink because their parents do not drink. They have been taught not to turn to alcohol. Others do not drink because of their religious beliefs. Some don't drink because they don't have the money to buy alcohol, or their health is bad. Some do not like the way liquor tastes, or what it does to them. Some are fearful of what alcohol will do to them mentally, physically, and spiritually. Some do not drink because of the nature of their work. And others do not drink because they know they will die if they use alcohol any longer. Some do not drink because of who they are. If you are a young person, I would say, "Tell me who your heroes are, what they do, and how they live, and I'll tell you who you are."

Who do you admire? Who do you want to be like? What do you want to be? If you admire great people, statesmen, writers, artists, surgeons, scientists, musicians, Olympic champions—and if you have constructive goals toward which you are working—your chances of becoming a fine person are excellent.

But if you have a sneaking admiration for criminals who

don't get caught; for notorious people with unsavory personal lives; for students who are always playing hooky, drinking, shooting dope, and being nonconformists—then you had better overhaul your thinking before it is too late.

Take a long, hard look at anyone who offers to decide what your life should be. Remember you are the one who will have to pay the consequences for that decision. If you let others decide for you, you may begin a way of life which will bring you suffering, pain, hurt, and failure throughout your life.

Decision making is a process of selecting the best course of action out of all the possible alternatives of life. To develop a sense of personal standards that will measure the best in life, you might want to study value clarification. This process will help you identify your own personal values and clarify them in order to make more intelligent and life-fulfilling decisions about the problems facing you.

The sources of your values include your family, your friends, and your peers, as well as your environment—your school, your church, place of work, social clubs, and athletic teams. If you can't get along with your teachers, your parents, your brothers and sisters, your peers who have high ideals and noble ambitions, take a long, hard look at yourself. Don't rely on those who would mislead you.

Life has much in store for you—the joy of achievement, the companionship of friends, the delight of love, marriage, and parenthood. All of these add up to infinite satisfaction. Alcohol abuse, by contrast, is a short-term thrill which can bring only untold suffering and degradation.

Yet the decision is yours. No matter how rough the waters of your life may be, remember the ship will never sink unless the water gets inside.

To the parents of young persons, I would emphasize that the most effective inoculation against alcohol abuse and other antisocial behaviors for your children is you and your home. Parents must face the hard truth. They set the stage for their kids to be drug abusers, because it is in the home that children learn what is good for themselves, their family, and society. Parents condition their children with their own thinking about alcohol, their failure to love their kids, their neglect in teaching the real values in life. Children acquire a sense of value from happy and loving relationships with their parents and by the standards that surround them.

Children who have been equipped with healthy methods of decision making and problem solving, who have been taught to accept responsibility for their actions, will not likely turn to alcohol to avoid or escape decisions, problems, and responsibilities.

What I am really talking about here is not just alcohol or alcohol abuse. What I am saying is that children must be taught the business of living. They must learn to deal with the reality of life, disappointments, and heartbreaks, because they live in an imperfect world with people who have faults. But they do not have to turn to a chemical to deal with the world's deficiencies.

That is why I am convinced that every child should be given a faith in God. Children and youth almost certainly will make mistakes, but if they have been given a healthy religion that helps them to relate to other persons and to God, as we know Him in Jesus Christ, they will be much more able to cope with the imperfections that life offers them.

Other adults besides parents have a role to play. There are teachers, ministers, the church members. The very least we can all do is to point out a way by being good examples. We must be consistent in what we say and supportive by the way we live. The old saying, "Do as I say, and not what I do," will not work for young people today.

Our youth are the strength of our nation. American young

people who are fine, responsible, and bighearted can create a world of hope and freedom, the kind of place in which we all want to live.

But the teenage years bring glandular changes, increased excitability, and emotional instability that make our young people easy pickings for any who would mislead them. Children and teenagers need help in finding healthy outlets for their emotions and in acquiring wholesome goals.

We must look at ways in which we can change the increasing use of alcohol among young people. If we do not, we are in for real trouble tomorrow.

What can we do? While basic information regarding alcohol and its effects on the body, mind, and spirit cannot act as an absolute deterrent to young people, still I am confident that such education is a good first step. Certainly there are a lot of misleading, false tales now being spread around among young persons.

The basic information about alcohol which I am including in the next chapter should be studied by both adults and youth.

12

How Alcohol Affects
the Body, Mind, and Spirit

One morning I visited a young man who had been hospitalized for alcoholism. Although just a teenager, he had been undergoing treatment for quite some time. Now, lying pale and weakened on his bed, he began to realize what alcohol had done to him. As the doctor stood behind me this young man had some important questions to ask.

"I've just made such an awful mess of my life!" he said. "Do you think my parents can ever forgive me?"

"Yes," I said. "I'm sure they will." He thought about this a moment, and then he had other questions.

"What about my friends? Will they forgive me too?"

"Yes, I know they will," I said.

"But what about God? Does He really forgive me for all of this?"

"Yes, God forgives you," I said.

Suddenly the doctor, who was standing behind me, broke in.

"Yes, all of these will forgive you. But your body cannot," he pointed out. "You are now seventeen years old, but you have the body of a forty-year-old man. The damage to your nervous system and your brain will never be forgiven."

If my young friend had known the terrible effects of alcohol, would he have become an alcoholic? There is no assurance that he would not. Yet I believe that if children could begin to study about alcohol in the fifth or sixth grade, many could avoid this heartbreak.

Some of the clearest and most concisely written information I have found on the effects of alcohol is in an instructor's guide for peer education compiled by Dick Upchurch, regional director of Southwest Allied Youth; Deanna French, Ph.D.; and Cole Murphy, Ph.D. Many schools throughout Texas and Canada are already using it. Some of the information I am including in this chapter is based on their work.

First of all, one should look at how the body uses or disposes of alcohol. It can basically be understood by examining the process called *metabolism,* or the way in which the body uses or disposes of food.

The means by which the metabolism of alcohol is accomplished in the human body is called *absorption.* The foods we eat have to be digested before being absorbed by the intestines, but alcohol does not. Alcohol is one of the few foods which is ready for absorption when it enters the stomach.

You should not be misled into thinking that alcohol is a good food. A *food* is anything that people consume for the purpose of nourishing and sustaining the body in its growth, health, and strength. Food provides various things—heat energy or fuel, body-building elements in the form of proteins and minerals, and those subtle chemical structures known as vitamins.

Good and wholesome foods that provide energy, strength, and growth to the body contain nutrients that can be stored as reserves and used in the future when needed by the body. Alcohol can be classified as a food because it has calories, or heat energy; but it is *not* a healthy food, because it does not provide energy for growth and health. Its energy cannot be stored in the body.

If a person who has taken in several hundred calories from alcohol continues to eat a normal diet, he will gain weight, since the calories derived from alcohol will be burned and the calories derived from food will be stored. The people who do not have the ability to store up fat will lose weight when they are drinking. They can even eat and drink, yet suffer malnutrition. This condition is especially harmful for young people, who have a special need for the kind of food that will build their bodies.

The chemical makeup of alcohol is simple enough to enable the body to use it for fuel almost immediately after swallowing it. The simple chemical structure of alcohol makes absorption much quicker than for most foods, because it can pass through the walls of the stomach and intestines very easily, without having to change. The walls of these organs are lined with tiny blood vessels called *capillaries*. The alcohol is absorbed through the stomach or intestinal walls directly into these tiny vessels. Within a matter of seconds after a few sips, the level of alcohol in the blood is raised to detectable levels.

Nevertheless it becomes very difficult to predict the effects of alcohol on an individual, because there are a number of factors that influence the rate at which alcohol is absorbed and used by the body of a particular person.

The size of the body of the drinker has an effect on the physical reaction to drinking. For example, the greater the body weight of the drinker, the larger the amount of alcohol required to significantly change the alcohol level in the blood. The larger body simply contains more body liquid with which to dilute the alcohol.

After a hundred-pound young adult drinks an ounce of alcohol, the concentration of alcohol in the blood would be approximately six percent. For a two-hundred-pound adult, the concentration of alcohol in the blood would be closer to only three percent after drinking an ounce. While these figures are averages and would be dependent on all other physical and emotional factors being the same in both persons, still they indicate that the two-hundred-pounder would require twice as much alcohol to get the same effect that a one-hundred-pounder gets.

Other factors which influence the rate at which alcohol is absorbed by a given individual are the type and amount of alcohol consumed and the length of time during which it is drunk. The greater the amount consumed, the longer it will take to be absorbed. The greater the amount of alcohol present in a drink, the quicker the alcohol is absorbed and the higher the alcohol level becomes in the blood. Drinking distilled liquors results in the highest blood-alcohol levels.

Another factor which has to be taken into consideration is the amount of chemicals other than alcohol in alcoholic beverages. The greater the amount of these nonalcoholic chemicals, the more slowly the alcohol is absorbed. Some of the nonalcoholic materials are salts, amino acids, vitamins, and other materials found in the mixes and juices used to dilute the drink.

For instance beer and wines contain more of these nonalcoholic chemicals than the distilled liquors, so they are absorbed at a lower rate. For this reason many people think they can drink beer and wine without really being affected, but the truth is that they are affected. Alcohol is alcohol, regardless of what it is wrapped in.

Food is another very important factor that affects the absorption. When you take alcohol with food or drink following a meal, the absorption rate is reduced.

One of the worst customs Americans have is drinking before meals. Thus the alcoholic intake is absorbed much more rapidly than if they drank following a meal. This is especially true in reference to wine.

Many experienced drinkers make such statements as "I

never drink on an empty stomach," or "I won't have more than one drink before dinner." These people are aware of the fact that the effects of an alcoholic drink are felt more rapidly on an empty stomach than during or after a meal. If you drink while you eat, it does not mean that you do not become intoxicated. It merely means that the absorption is slowed down. It takes the body longer to sort out the alcohol.

Another factor which influences the rate of absorption is the rate at which you consume alcohol. By drinking alcohol rapidly or in gulps, the rate of absorption can also be raised more quickly than if you sip it. Blood-alcohol levels will be lower after sipping a drink than after gulping the same drink.

Absorption also seems to be speeded up when the stomach empties more rapidly than normal. The reduction or increase of the emptying time for the stomach may be caused by fear, stress, anger, or nausea.

After alcohol has been absorbed, how is it distributed in the body? Absorbed in the bloodstream, alcohol is greatly diluted in the circulating body fluids. The alcohol in the blood reaches all the organs in the body and probably has some effect on most of them. It takes a smaller concentration of alcohol to produce effects on the brain than it takes to cause a similar change on other organs and tissues. The effect of alcohol on the brain is what determines the behavior of the person who has been drinking.

Since it is during the time that alcohol is being circulated through the body that changes in behavior occur, this time period is not when you should be making decisions about drinking. Once you've had too much to drink, you may not be able to decide when you should stop or what you should do.

Now let us look at the effects of alcohol on the various organs of the body, and we shall see why the doctor told my young friend that his body could never forgive him for the long periods of alcoholism which he had inflicted on it.

Drunkenness refers to the progressive effects of an increase in alcohol in the blood. As the percentage of alcohol increases, the effects on the body become more serious. The effects progress from the disturbance of sense organs (a decrease in muscular control combined with the loss of intelligent behavior) to eventual unconsciousness and death. One can become drunk very quickly, but sobering up is a slow process. And, as heavy drinkers know, sobering up can be painful. The hangover or morning-after symptoms of drinking include nausea, headaches, and sensitivity to noise.

People have the idea that if they do not have a hangover, alcohol has not affected them. But one of the things that we find as a sign of being in trouble with alcohol very early in life is that the person involved in this kind of problem often does not experience any hangover.

Alcohol in the system slows down the responses of the hands, the eyes, and the feet; even hearing is impaired. If you've ever been watching a football game with a group of people who are drinking, you may have noticed that, as the game and drinking both progressed, invariably the drinkers wanted to turn the volume louder. Alcohol reduces one's ability to hear.

Alcohol is popularly believed to have a warming effect on the body, since it increases the flow of blood to the skin. In reality, the expansion of the small blood vessels in the skin due to alcohol in the blood permits larger quantities of blood to flow closer to the skin and to lose body heat.

The body attempts to control its temperature by the position of the blood supply in much the same way that a couple does when living in an un-air-conditioned house in the summer. To cool off they move closer to the window, just as the blood moves closer to the skin. But if it is cold outside, in order to be warmer they move away from the window to the interior of the house.

On a cold morning you will notice that you can hardly see the blood vessels on the back of your hand because the blood has moved to the interior, keeping your body temperature as warm as possible. On a hot day your blood vessels will be very obvious, because they will enlarge and allow the blood to move to the outer part of your body in order to make your body feel cooler.

But the use of alcohol throws this body air-conditioning system out of kilter. Drinking alcohol in cold weather can be dangerous.

What else does alcohol affect? Alcohol is an irritant to the delicate lining of the throat and esophagus. It burns as it goes down the "food pipe." But it is the liver that is most severely affected by alcohol, because it has more responsibility for processing alcohol than any other organ.

Research shows that little or no damage is caused to a healthy liver by moderate drinking. Extensive drinking for long periods of time, however, frequently leads to seriously impaired liver functions. Some liver disorders associated with alcohol are fatty livers, alcohol hepatitis, and alcohol cirrhosis. There still exists some heated discussion as to whether hepatitis and cirrhosis are direct results of alcohol consumption or whether they are caused by malnutrition or foreign particles associated with alcoholic beverages.

The fact remains that heavy drinkers have proportionately more problems with these diseases than do nondrinkers or moderate drinkers. It seems that alcohol inflames the cells of the liver, causing them to swell and block the tiny canals to the small intestines. Hence bile cannot be filtered properly through the liver. Each drink of alcohol increases the number of liver cells destroyed, eventually causing cirrhosis of the liver; so this disease is many times more frequent among alcoholics than nonalcoholics.

The heart may also be affected by drinking. Even small amounts of alcohol may be dangerous for someone with heart problems, because the presence of alcohol in the blood increases circulation and stress on the heart muscles. For those who drink excessively over long periods of time, heart problems can result.

Alcohol causes inflammation of the heart muscles. It has a toxic effect on the heart and causes an increased amount of fat to collect. Thus it disrupts the normal metabolism. People suffering from heart damage resulting from alcohol intake can recover when treated as any other heart patient if they practice abstinence from alcoholic beverages.

What happens to the stomach and intestines? Drinking stimulates acid production, which results in irritation of the stomach lining. In addition alcohol delays the normal emptying of the stomach. This causes the food, excess gastric juices, and acids to remain in the stomach longer than usual —compounding the problem.

The nonalcoholic contents of the drink may also cause digestive upsets. The combination of two or more alcoholic beverages may irritate the stomach much as do certain combinations of food. Although a person may experience digestive upsets by drinking combinations of alcoholic beverages (such as changing from beer to bourbon in the same evening), there is no difference in the risk of intoxication. Vomiting and nausea are quite common following excessive drinking, especially for those who drink infrequently.

Many heavy drinkers are poorly nourished because their excessive drinking irritates the lining of their stomachs. These people simply lose their desire to eat. The general health of such persons suffers because they are drinking alcohol instead of eating food which would provide them with the necessary vitamins, minerals, and proteins.

Many people believe that the kidneys are damaged by alcohol because of the increased frequency of urination following drinking. This increase is caused by the action of alcohol on the pituitary gland rather than on the kidneys. The secretion from the pituitary gland regulates the amount of liquid removed from the body by the kidneys. However, the kidneys may also be affected, because alcohol causes increased loss of fluid through its irritating effects. Alcohol also inflames the lining of the urinary bladder, making it unable to stretch properly.

Drinking can also cause sexual impotence. Modern research has conclusively established that alcohol reverses the normal physical and mental functions in the human body. Research teams in government medical centers such as those at Bethesda, Maryland, and Pittsburgh have made extensive tests that offer conclusive evidence that a man who uses an alcoholic beverage over a considerable length of time may become hopelessly impotent. All indications are that alcohol may affect the female as much as the male, by attacking her nervous system.

Unfortunately, once the nervous centers of any part of the body are damaged, most medical research seems to agree that repair is not likely. Many of the organs of the body do repair themselves. But once the nervous system has been damaged by alcohol, it does not repair itself.

The principal effect of alcohol on the body is in the brain. The most dramatic and noticeable effect of alcohol excess is the depression of the brain center, producing progressive incoordination, confusion, disorientation, stupor, coma, and even death. Alcohol no doubt kills brain cells, and the brain damage is permanent. The brain cannot grow new cells. Hence drinking over a period of time causes loss of memory, judgment, and learning ability.

Anyone considering this subject should also realize that alcohol affects one's behavioral patterns. Everyone who drinks does not exhibit the same outward behavior pattern, of course. Some people become loud and boisterous; others become quiet. After one or two drinks another person or even this same person may consume considerably more but display no outward effects. The reason is that people can learn to control their outward behavior after drinking if they feel strongly enough that they should. The important point to consider is that there is no way of telling how much a person has been drinking or how much his brain has been influenced by alcohol simply by observing his outward moves or behavior.

The amount of the brain that is affected by alcohol depends on the blood-alcohol level. The first parts of the brain to be influenced are the nerve centers controlling the higher functions that involve learning. The last nerve center to be influenced is that controlling the automatic body functions, such as breathing. For this reason one of the first behavioral effects of alcohol relates to judgment and inhibitions.

What are our inhibitions? The restraints or brakes that people learn to apply to control their normal behavior are their *inhibitions*. These are not characteristics with which we are born. Inhibitions must be learned. For example very young children are characteristically very selfish persons. When they see a toy they want, they see no reason why they shouldn't have it. If they are refused, they become very upset. They may sulk, pout, or become angry. Eventually, however, they learn through example (and through their parents' sometimes strenuous training program) that some items do not belong to them. The children leave these toys alone because they have learned to inhibit their natural reactions.

Much more sophisticated inhibitions are learned by individuals as new problems are faced. By young adulthood we have learned inhibitions that restrain the behavior we exhibit in most of our social contacts. By this age we are very conscious of the fact that we must tender our behavior according to the people with whom we are associated.

These restraints or inhibitions are learned so well and prac-
ticed so often that they become a part of our behavior.

Not all persons are as restrained as others. Many practice
certain restraints because they know that certain behavior
patterns are expected of them. But they never learn to feel
comfortable with them. Other persons are so concerned by
what people think of them that they are uncomfortable
when they are in a group. For such persons, alcohol becomes an escape from inhibitions that lock them into discomfort. They can relax because they are no longer concerned with restraining their behavior. They become more
active, talk more freely, and generally feel more at ease.

It is easy to see that most people tend to talk more and
listen less after a few drinks. Many do a great deal of interrupting of others' conversations. They pay little or no attention to what others are saying. There is no doubt that alcohol may "loosen up" people, but certainly it also causes
them to become more disorganized, and the rules of
etiquette seem to get lost.

Although such drinkers appear to be stimulated by alcohol when they are exhibiting this behavior, what really
occurs is that their inhibitions have been released. Like a
car going downhill without brakes, such people are heading
for trouble.

Muscular control is also changed by the consumption of
alcohol. The length of time that elapses between the brain's
receiving a signal and the body's response is greater than
usual. Many people mistakenly believe that alcohol in any
amount increases the efficiency of many kinds of physical
performances. This idea probably stems from the fact that
consumption of alcohol creates a sense of well-being which
may lead to overconfidence, an inflated ego, or the willingness to take a foolish chance. But in actuality muscular
coordination required for skillful manipulation is hampered
by alcohol. Drinking delays reaction time.

Now let us see how the body disposes of alcohol, a process that is called *oxidation*. This breaking down of alcohol is begun by enzymes in the liver. Because large bodies have larger livers than small ones, a larger person probably will oxidize alcohol faster than a smaller one.

After most foods are eaten, the body can speed up the rate of oxidation, but not after drinking alcohol. Nothing has been found to speed the rate at which alcohol leaves the body and loses its effect.

The widely held belief that hot coffee, exercise, fresh air, cold showers, hot baths, or shock sobers a person or nullifies the effects of alcohol has been proved to be false.

The symptoms of drinking alcohol only become less pronounced as the concentration of alcohol in the blood becomes lower. The effects of all the old-time remedies listed above may make a person feel more wide-awake or alert, but the symptoms are still there.

Another factor in disposing of alcohol is that of elimination. The speed with which alcohol is removed from the body depends on the individual, his size, his age, and the condition of his liver. The liver has the task of removing the alcohol from the blood. This job is performed at the rate of about one ounce every two hours. About two percent to ten percent of the alcohol consumed is eliminated through the urine, the breath, and perspiration. Alcohol eliminated in this manner has not been broken down by the body.

Without a doubt the entire body is affected by the use of alcohol. After much study, one can reach the conclusion that drinking does not add to one's health or physical well-being. Prolonged use of alcohol may permanently injure one's body, mind, and spirit.

13

A New Life

The hour is late, and David is tossing on his bed. His wife, Jane, is awake in another room. Neither can sleep because they are thrashing their brains for an answer about what to do. Their problem stems from the sickish odor of alcohol permeating their home. Even though every room is luxuriously furnished and there is a late-model car in the driveway, both know that there is no money in their bank account to cover the latest checks David has written. There is not even very much food in the kitchen.

David writhes on his bed. He tries to pray. Instead he ends up cursing. All he can think of are his regrets, the recurring body sweats, his shame, and his humiliation. There is no doubt about it. He has to do something about his drinking. If he doesn't, he has reached the end.

David has heard about "surrender," a word he knows has something to do with how religion is supposed to help when things are the darkest. But how does he surrender? He's tried to pray, and he can't. He thinks of the rubber checks he has written, and the suffering his family will experience because of them, and remorse overcomes him.

"Jane, Jane," he calls out in the darkness. His wife comes and stands rigidly in the doorway to the darkened hall.

"What do you want now?" she asks. Her voice is cold and hard.

"Please, Jane, please help me," David says. He feels the

tears welling up in his eyes. "I've tried everything, and nothing seems to work."

"Well, what do you want me to do about it?"

"I want you to call your minister," David says. "Maybe he can do something for me."

"My minister? Do you think I'd call him at this time of the night to come out here and see you like this?" With shaking hands, Jane slams the door shut. "Good night!" comes her parting shot.

But now, as Jane sobs on her bed, her husband's words continue to ring in her ears for a long time. "Call your minister. Maybe he can help," David had said. *This is the first time in all the miserable days since he has started drinking that he has ever asked to see a minister. Could this be the solution?* Jane slips on a robe and tiptoes into David's bedroom. She finds him still sitting on the side of the bed, shivering in his striped pajamas, his head in his hands. She kneels beside him and takes his hands in her own.

"I'm sorry about what I said a moment ago," she says. "I'll call my minister right now."

But David shakes his head. "No, it's after midnight. Let's wait until morning."

"But it may be too late then. My minister won't mind. Let's call him now," Jane pleads.

Driving through the darkened streets to their house, I am glad that Jane has called, for I already know the misery that David has been experiencing. I can't help but think of how the Prodigal Son rehearsed a repentant speech when he decided to call on his father for help. "I'm no more worthy to be called thy son: make me as one of thy hired servants," he was going to say, but his father never let him voice the words. Instead, just as soon as he saw him coming back, the father put a robe on his son's back, which is a symbol of distinction; a ring on his finger for a mark of authority; and shoes on his feet to remove the symbol of the barefoot slave (*see* Luke 15:19–22).

The way Jane had talked over the phone, David seems to be feeling just as repentant. And I want him to experience the same kind of supporting love. But am I the one who will be able to present it to him? As I drive, I alternate between wishing that someone would tell me what to do for this desperate man and rehearsing the speech I am going to make about the Prodigal Son. But as soon as I walk in the door I realize that I am never going to make that speech. Something new has been introduced in David, even if he does not know it; and that *something* is God. David begins to pour out his heart to me.

"I don't know what's wrong with me," he begins. "I was raised in a good Christian home and exposed to a good education. But in college I began to drink because it seemed the popular thing to do. Alcohol helped me become the life of the party. It gave me a lift when I was down. I felt a real warmth from drink, and I could take it or leave it then. I developed a good business, a large organization. I had more money than I knew what to do with, and not a single financial trouble.

"And then, all of a sudden, I started drinking more and more heavily. I'm an independent sort of guy. When people tried to advise me to lay off the liquor, I told them I didn't need anyone's advice on anything. I drank more and more. I became arrogant and selfish. I knew I was that way, but I couldn't seem to stop it. The only thing that mattered to me was to get everything I could. I never thought about giving anything to anybody else.

"Now look at me. I'm scared to death, and I'm being insulted and humiliated every day. I've neglected my family. I don't know how they put up with me.

"I've lost my business. We have no income. We're about to lose our home. We have no food in the house, and my health is wrecked. Yet all I can do is walk around in a drunken stupor—like this." Now David looks straight at me.

"Preacher, I've never been a religious man, but I've prayed to God about this," he says, slurring his words. "I told God that if He would keep me from drinking, I'd go back to church. I'd do anything. But He didn't stop me from drinking." David stares at me reproachfully a second, then turns away mumbling. "I'm not really surprised. I never have really believed in God. I don't have any faith. I'd like to believe, but I just really don't."

"David, all of us believe, all of us have faith in something," I say. "The question isn't *whether* you believe or *whether* you have faith. The question is *what* do you believe in? What do you put your faith in? Whatever you believe in and have faith in, that's what is going to direct your life. Apparently you have believed in alcohol. You have put your faith and trust in it, and alcohol has not kept faith with you."

"Preacher, I'm so sick."

"I'll tell you what, let's try to get you sober."

"No, no, I can't wait to get sober. I've got to talk about this right now," he insists.

"All right," I say, "how can I help you?" David squirms a bit and then bites his lip.

"I've heard about making an unconditional surrender. I've heard it helps, and I'm ready to do it if you think I should," he says point-blank.

I am both pleased and cautious when I hear those words. There is no doubt that David's willingness to surrender is an opportunity for him to receive help, but David is walking a tightrope now. If he can experience the new birth that Jesus has promised to all who are repentant and turn to Him, his life will become a wonderful thing. But the slightest misstep can throw him back into the depths of alcoholism. There are very real dangers for him at this crucial moment.

For while religion is in the business of redemption, it often seems to many on the receiving end that religion is merely another system of rejection and condemnation. All David has to do is hear about judgment rather than love, and he will turn away from this new beginning.

Often in the church we hear one person making an appeal for another because that individual is "worthy." But haven't we all done things that were less than what we might have done? And what about the unworthy individual? Perhaps the unworthy person is made that way because no one considers him worthy of help. The alcoholic has often been kicked out of church and turned off by religion because religious people have been very judgmental.

But those of us who are custodians of God's Word and work must realize that guilt and fear are not a deterrent to drinking. It is a tragic mistake to increase alcoholics' not-OK feelings (guilt and fear). By doing so we simply widen the gulf between them and God and their neighbors. We intensify the loneliness that their illness creates.

Since we must present God in such a way that alcoholics do not feel rejected, it is ineffective to scold, threaten or point out mistakes. David has already condemned himself enough. In fact I know I will have to be very careful not to inadvertently increase David's guilt feelings. I am quite sure that once David sobers up he will feel very uncomfortable in the presence of a minister or a religious group. Not only does he have feelings of guilt; he also has great fears of being punished.

Unless someone convinces David of the mercy and goodness of God, there is no hope for him. David needs to receive the reinstatement of himself back into the family to which he rightly belongs, just as did the Prodigal Son. But we must start with David where he is, with what he believes, even though for the time being he is rejecting his beliefs—or trying to do so.

As Ernest Campbell once said, "In the life of faith, there may be guides, but there can be no proxies." David must come to believe for himself, not as I believe. Because David has said he is ready to make a complete surrender, I have a good place to start helping him. But at the same time, I know there is one thing that most alcoholics cannot stand, and that is the urgency of being saved. Just as a fruit tree cannot be rushed into producing and bearing fruit, so the soul must be allowed to face itself in its quest for God.

To prey on the fears of alcoholics, to use failure or death as a lever, to push for an instant commitment or decision is wrong. David needs to experience the new birth that Nicodemus sought when he came to Jesus in the night.

Nicodemus said to Jesus, ". . . Rabbi, we know that you are a teacher come from God; for no one can do these signs that you do, unless God is with him" (John 3:2).

Jesus addressed his problem directly and quickly. He said, ". . . Truly, truly, I say to you, unless one is born anew, he cannot see the kingdom of God" (John 3:3). No doubt that statement set Nicodemus back on his heels. He was not ready for that. But he recovered quickly, asking a question of Jesus.

"How can a man be born when he is old? Can he enter a second time into his mother's womb and be born?" (John 3:4). Jesus made it clear to Nicodemus that this was another kind of birth, a spiritual beginning somewhat comparable to that of the physical birth.

Is there any way that I might help David experience the new life in the Spirit that Jesus described? I cannot abandon my own religious beliefs, but I must start where David is. I have to offer him milk for babes and not meat for the adult, realizing that milk is also nourishing. The ingredients that I have to share with David are my faith in Jesus Christ, the reality of forgiveness, the effectiveness of prayer, and the knowledge of what it means to be born again.

I believe that David not only can understand what it means to be born again; he can accept it if I present it in terms of a new life. For this is what David seeks. He realizes, subconsciously perhaps, that it is necessary for his rehabilitation.

But during our discussion I find that it is difficult to keep controversial discussion and hairsplitting out of the conversation. I have to be very careful to stay with basic religion.

Now David is asking me a very important question.

"What does surrender mean, anyway?"

"David, it's like what you have done with alcohol," I say. "Alcohol has been your god. You have turned over every waking hour to it. You cannot think of life without it. It consumes your total being. This is what complete surrender means.

"What we need to do is help you make this same kind of commitment to a new way of life, to a new God, as we know Him in Jesus Christ. Are you willing to give to Him the same kind of commitment in terms of time, energy, thought, and feelings? Are you willing to place in Him the same kind of faith, trust, and confidence that you have in alcohol? If you are, then you will find a new birth, a new life." David looks worried.

"I don't know," he says, "I'm not sure I am able to do that." I point out to him that the greatest gift God has given to us as human beings is our ability to adjust our attitude in relation to our changing needs.

"But everything I once had is gone—my money, my business. I don't even seem to have any willpower left. I don't have anything left to change."

"But David," I say, "your success in life is not dependent on what you have or how much you have. If you will just take what you do have and turn it all over to God, you'll be surprised at what He can do with it."

David's attitude points up the fact that most alcoholics fail more from their inability to change than from the fact that they have a disease. If David can make this change of attitude, he can experience total surrender.

Yet I know there are a lot of pitfalls in surrendering. I have to be sure that David will not abuse religion as he once abused alcohol. He must not substitute one crutch for another. Shallow and ill-founded religious beliefs must not consume and destroy our lives, our thoughts, our acts, and our jobs. We must make sure that religion does not become just another escape for David.

Of course it would be equally detrimental if David waits until he is on his deathbed before he decides to call on God for help; though obviously it is better to call on Him even at the last minute then never to do it at all.

It seems that some people must be faced with a crisis before they become aware of their need for religion. But these people should not be allowed to react with a crash program. What they need is a day-to-day participation in a new relationship with God. I see that David is taking in everything I have to say.

"Do I really have any hope of bringing about the change that is needed in my life?" he asks.

"Yes, David, you do," I assure him. I remind him that someone once asked Albert Schweitzer whether he was an optimist or a pessimist. The great medical missionary said that a large part of what he saw every day was material for pessimism, but by his faith and work he was largely an optimist.

Even if what David and I see in him is material for pessimism, we can apply faith and work optimistically.

"Well, will God get me out of this mess, then?" David asks.

I have to answer honestly. "No, He won't, not without your help, not without your efforts. But if you will turn your life and will over to God, you will find strength beyond yourself," I say.

Here again I must be careful not to paint too rosy a picture for David, or lead him to believe that someone else will solve all his problems for him.

"The Bible tells us that God is our refuge and strength, and a very present help in time of trouble," I say. "With God on our side, no one needs to go down into defeat. And that means *no one*.

"You see, David, the first and greatest commandment is that '. . . you shall love the Lord your God with all your heart, and with all your soul, and with all your mind, and with all your strength,' and when you do this, something will happen. But religion has not been helpful to a lot of people, because we've led them to believe that all they have to do is come to the altar of the church and leave their burdens and sins for God to take care of. I wish it were that easy.

"One of the beautiful things about AA is that they invite people in and put around them a sense of caring, concern, and love. And they introduce them to a program of rehabilitation. But to receive the program you have to learn to go out and give it away."

David looks very disappointed when I say that.

"It sounds to me as if you're saying I've got to give something to others before I can get the kind of life I want. How can I do that? I've spent my life getting, not giving," he says.

"But the paradox is that we do get strength by giving. Before God is willing to give to us, we have to give God our heart, our soul, our mind, our strength," I say.

I have to point out that there is no way that God can remove the pain that David will experience in sobering up. God can heal, but He cannot remove the scars. God cannot remove the consequences of David's failure—his broken relationships, the lack of trust which has developed in friends and employees. But God *can* give him the strength to handle them.

Bishop John Vincent has said it this way, "Reach up as far as you can and God will reach down the rest of the way." Put another way, when you reach the end of your rope and feel your strength is running out, just tie a knot in it and hold on. But always know that God has hold of the other end.

Still another nugget of wisdom which I came across in a professional trade journal put it this way: "We make a living by what we get, and we make a life by what we give." David must be able to understand what it is to be forgiven by God, others, and himself. Then he will receive strength to give.

If you go back and read the story of the crucifixion, you will find that while Jesus was on the cross, suffering the inhumanity of one man to another, He said, ". . . Father, forgive them, for they know not what they do" (Luke 23:34). When Jesus uttered these words, it was God's way of saying to us, "I forgive you, won't you please accept My forgiveness?"

But it is difficult to get alcoholics to accept forgiveness. We must help them to discover that they are not just drunkards and no-good bums, but children of God. Once they discover that God really does want them in His family, they approach life with a different kind of attitude.

As one old country preacher put it, "The crucifixion was God's way of saying 'I ain't mad at you; I accept you.' " While the illness of alcoholism has caused many people to do things that they are ashamed of, God wants them to know that they are still worthwhile. They are somebody important.

I have heard it said that yesterday is a canceled check; tomorrow is a promissory note; and today is ready cash.

We may be surprised to find out how much our canceled checks total, but we can't unwrite them. If we continue to dwell on yesterday's mistakes and refuse to accept God's grace and forgive ourselves, we can totally ruin today.

Neither do we have any way of knowing whether tomorrow's promissory notes will be paid. They may never come due for some of us. And often a promissory note matures at a far different sum than what we had hoped.

All we really have is today, our ready cash. We can spend it as we will. Use today, then, as if it were your most precious possession. Don't waste it in regretting what you did yesterday or dreaming of what you will do tomorrow. Accept the forgiveness of wasted yesterdays and live today in God's forgiveness. In a sense, all of our lives are composed of what we do in a continuing present. Today takes on a significance when we realize that we are most alive right now.

Psalm 118 says, "This is the day which the Lord has made; let us rejoice and be glad in it" (v. 24). God's forgiveness cleans away the rubbish and gives us a chance to truly live today. In fact today is the measure of our intelligence and our personal discipline.

Most of my ministry has been spent in building or remodeling church plans. Many a church architect has helped me resolve the problems involved in remodeling an old building. When a building has grown like Topsy, its greatest problem has been to make all the changes fit into a logical and attractive whole. It takes far greater skill and infinitely more patience to remodel an old building than it does to construct a new one.

Life is much the same, especially for alcoholics. Each of us evidences some amount of confusion and poor planning. We all have habits and expressions that grow on us and illnesses that develop within us. We never intended that these liabilities should become the major part of our lives, but there they are, securely fastened onto us. They are a part of us; we know that. And the alcoholic knows it.

Try as we might, we just don't seem to see any lovely and appealing solution for ourselves. We never will until the Great Architect of Life is approached, and we learn that He has a plan for us. Jesus Christ came to specialize in remaking the spoiled lives of people. He came to bring healing to the sick, to call the careless, the thoughtless, the headstrong, the willful into a new life of forgiveness and wholeness. He can show us how to get rid of the bad and how to salvage the good in our lives. He has the greatest remodeling plan of anyone I know. But you cannot accept that plan until you feel that you are forgiven. Only then can reconstruction begin.

Saint Louis of Granada has written: "He who goes to the sea to fetch water takes as much as the vessel he carries can contain. There is an abundance of water in the sea, which is an infinite abyss, but he will have only according to the greatness of the vessel he carries."

There is no lack of God's grace, and we will have it according to our capacity to hold it. But if you have not accepted forgiveness, there will be no room for either God's grace or His help.

". . . my cup runneth over," says the Twenty-third Psalm. It is simply another way of saying that we know that there is more of God's goodness for us than we can hold. The problem is not God's goodness, grace, or love. There is an abundance of all that. The problem is in our vessel. If we do not accept forgiveness, there will be no room for God's mercy.

Be assured that God will give liberally to all who ask Him in faith and sincere need. Like the Prodigal Son, we may have wandered away, but God wants us back—and not as self-deprecating, self-incriminating human beings with low self-esteem. God wants His children back repentant but feeling forgiven. David must come to know that God loves him, and that there are those around him who love him, regardless of how he feels or what he has done.

"But I haven't been to church or Sunday school since I was a little boy," David is saying. "How do you know that Jesus still loves me?"

"I can tell you why," I answer him. "Do you remember that song you used to sing as a child? 'Jesus loves me! this I know, For the Bible tells me so . . . ,' it goes. And I don't care what you've done as an alcoholic, there is no way you can get outside of God's love. You may not accept it, but God's love is there for you. God sent His only Son, Jesus Christ, to live among us and to die, so that He could show us how much He loved us."

I once heard a story about a lady whose father had purchased a ticket for her, so she could take an ocean voyage around the world. This woman knew that her father had sacrificed all he had in order to pay for the ticket, and she had very little money to spend on herself. "I'll just scrimp as much as I can," she thought.

When the other passengers went to the dining room to eat the wonderful meals they raved about, she went to her cabin and ate a sandwich or the crackers and cheese she had stowed away in her luggage. But on the last day of the voyage, she decided to splurge. She went to the dining room for lunch and ordered all her favorite dishes. Everything was delicious, and she was delighted. But when she asked for the check, she found there was no charge. The ticket which her father had bought included the price of every mouth-watering meal she had missed during the whole voyage! She had been living on dry bread, crackers, and cheese when she might have had the most luxurious meals.

The moral of this story is plain. Many of us live on a spiritual diet of dry bread and cheese when we could be feasting on God's love. We are undernourished and lonely at the same time that God would have us know that His table is spread out before us. He will fill our cup to over-flowing if we but hold it out before Him.

So quit beating yourself down and feeling you are no good. God wants to bless you. All you have to do is take Him at His word. The free gift of God's love is life, life today.

"But how can I learn to trust God's love?" David asks.

"David, the individual who wants to learn trust must be placed in a relationship with somebody else who is trusting," I say. "Perhaps you find yourself in the presence of a wife, a minister, or someone else who you know cares for you and loves you. If you do, you can start on your journey toward trusting God because of this relationship. God reveals Himself as one whose love can be trusted through others."

"But how will I know when God loves me, and when I love God?"

"You will know it for many reasons," I say. "But one indication is the direction in which your life points. Will it turn to that which is God, or will it point to the drug, alcohol? The needle of a compass is so delicately balanced that the least little jolt will cause it to turn and twist. When you pick up a compass, the needle quivers and turns. But if you hold it still, it will always come to rest pointing toward the magnetic north. In this way it is a dependable guide for the one wanting to know directions.

"By the same token the people who love God are attracted to the magnetic person of Christ. They always come to rest pointing to Him, the values He has demonstrated, and the love He portrays."

Each one of us too should be aware of the magnetic poles of the things or ideas that attract us. Unerringly, the individuals for whom money is everything will point their lives' efforts at financial gains. Alcoholics will aim everything at the drinking crowd. People who have turned their lives and wills over to the love of God will reveal their magnetic poles by the things they say and do each day.

Of course, the godly person may have moments of unfaithfulness. The money-driven man may burst out with an occasional bout of generosity. The alcoholic may ease into a period of sobriety. But once the movement of their compasses is stilled, they will always point to the true goal of their lives when they come to rest. If you keep your mind and heart on God's love today, you will know that you love God and that He will bless you.

There was once a young girl who lived in an orphanage, who was so unattractive and awkward, so dull in personality, and a troublemaker too that the superintendent and her staff just could not bear her. Because they knew that no one would ever want to adopt such an unfeminine little girl, they planned a way of getting rid of her. Day and night they watched her, encouraging her to make a mistake so that they would have a reason for recommending that she be sent to a reform school.

One day their chance came. Although the young people were forbidden to leave the grounds, a staff member saw her sneak out the front gate. She climbed a tree, crawled out on a limb, and tied a note to it with a piece of string. Then she climbed down and returned to the orphanage. The superintendent and a number of the staff ran to see what she had done. When the superintendent took the note and began to read it to herself, tears rolled down her hardened cheeks.

"What does it say?" demanded the others. She held it out for them to read.

"Whoever finds this note, I love you," it said.

God did a similar thing. He wrote a note on a tree outside the wall of Jerusalem at a place called Golgotha. In essence this is what He said, "Whoever finds My Son, you will know that I love you."

Before the night is over David asks me a very meaningful question. "What kind of God are you asking me to put my faith and trust in?" he asks.

"What do you mean, David?"

"I mean, you say God calls people. Do you think He calls me to be an alcoholic?"

"No, David, I think God is hurting, just as you are hurting. God didn't cause you to become an alcoholic, but He did grant you the freedom to become one. And God will not remove your compulsion to drink or your pain, but He will give you the strength to handle both if you will give Him your cooperation. Trust and have faith in God, because He gives and shares His love with us.

"Even though these gifts are unearned, undeserved, and unexpected, His love is already given to us and is available without price to each of us. He is not a God whose love is to be sought, then bought, but a God whose love is waiting to be truly accepted and used. He is not a God who cares for me in proportion to my love for Him, but a God who cares for me because of His unlimited love for me. His awareness of me is not bound by my past behavior or present performance. He is a God who also is aware of my potential and that which I can become. The God I believe in is one who will give me another chance.

"You know, David, God is not like those people who make sure who is calling on the phone before they decide to answer it. I admit I get a little irritated when I phone someone and am asked 'Who's calling?' and the next thing I know I am informed that that person is not in. These people seem to have telephone guards instructed to protect them from callers who will bother them. Ultimately it is up to the telephone guard to decide whether or not my call should get attention.

"Thank goodness, it isn't that way with God. Our intermediary is Jesus Christ; we do not have to wait until a convenient time to be heard.

"You may not get to talk to your doctor about your ills, your banker about your shortages, your merchants about your purchases, or your minister about your spiritual health. But you can speak to God without any interference whatsoever. He's waiting for your call. And when He calls you, it is not station to station, but person to person.

"God doesn't simply respond to our requests. He also initiates them so that we might respond to them. He's not a God who says to you, 'You've got to do this or that.' He's not going to say to you, 'David, you have to get sober.' And He won't make you get sober. But He does say to you, 'You may get sober, and with My help you can. I will strengthen you. Underneath are my Everlasting Arms.'

"No, David, God's not going to make everything easy, safe, comfortable, and sure. But He is a God who offers you a life of unlimited opportunities in the face of all the odds that are against you. He is a God who stands at the door and knocks. All you have to do is open it and greet Him. He is a loving God, not a judgmental one. He is a forgiving God who always forgets everything that He has given and shares with us His love and grace. To love Him means to accept His gifts through faith and trust. I owe my life and means to God, so I try to use my life and means for God."

As I once heard another say, "I give my life and means for those in need of God." This is the kingdom of God on earth as it is in heaven.

When a mason builds a brick wall, he uses his level on every new row to be sure the layers are even and the work is progressing straight. If a workman needs to check up on his handwork hour after hour without trusting his years of experience, doesn't it stand to reason that all of us should check up on ourselves as we go through life?

Recovering alcoholics especially need someone with whom they can check, and the church and AA certainly provide such reference points. For instance the big book of AA has its tools for seeing that your life is running on an even keel. In the big book of life, the Bible, Jesus Christ suggests some measuring sticks for your life. Do you have good thinking or bad thinking? Do you have healthy or sick thinking?

The parable of the Good Samaritan helps us measure our neighborliness. The Golden Rule applies to all relationships with others. The widow's mite reflects the kind of generosity that we need to have. Jesus' dying on the cross for man points the finger at the height of God's love and the path of unselfishness. His mercy leads us away from criticism to compassion. These and others are the tools which God uses to measure the span of our days and the heights of our living.

Yes, religion does help. Without it, many an alcoholic must paraphrase the Twenty-third Psalm in this way:

Alcohol is my shepherd, I shall want for ever;
   he makes me lie down in barren pastures.
He leads me beside rough water;
   he destroys my soul.
He leads me in the paths of wrongness,
   for his name's sake.

Even though I walk through the valley of illness and death,
   I will fear all good;
for thou art with me;
   thy compulsion and obsession,
   they torment me.

Thou preparest an empty table before me
   in the presence of my abundance;
thou anointest my head with pain,
   my misery overflows.

Surely hate and resentment shall follow me
    all the days of my living death;
and I shall dwell in the house of the forgotten
    for ever, unless I can find a different shepherd.

    How much more wonderful to be able to affirm, after surrendering to God and accepting His forgiveness, the words that so many recovering alcoholics have learned to say of themselves:

The Lord is my shepherd, I shall not want;
    he makes me lie down in green pastures.
He leads me beside still waters;
    he restores my soul.
He leads me in paths of righteousness
    for his name's sake.

Even though I walk through the valley of the shadow of
    death,
    I fear no evil;
for thou art with me;
    thy rod and thy staff,
    they comfort me.

Thou preparest a table before me
    in the presence of my enemies;
thou anointest my head with oil,
    my cup overflows.
Surely goodness and mercy shall follow me
    all the days of my life;
and I shall dwell in the house of the Lord
    for ever.

                                  Psalm 23

Publisher's Afterword

It was with great sadness that we learned, shortly before this book was to be released, that the Reverend Thomas J. Shipp had died suddenly of a heart attack. In the midst of his duties for his beloved Lovers Lane United Methodist Church, which he had pastored for almost thirty-two years, his work was ended without warning.

His congregation and the thousands of others whose lives he had touched mourned his passing. For, as United Methodist Bishop W, McFerrin Stowe said at his funeral services, "He poured his life out in an utterly magnificent way."

A large, imposing man, Tom Shipp was gentle and compassionate. When he was only six years old, his father had turned him out of his house in Missouri to face the world alone, with the explanation that he could no longer feed him. A farm family let him sleep in their barn and work in their fields for his keep. Later he and his younger brother lived together in a hut on the outskirts of town for three years, going to school and supporting themselves by hunting, trapping, and odd jobs.

These experiences might have embittered a different person. But in Tom Shipp, adversity created a better understanding of the hardships of others. It enabled him to transmit his deep faith in God and in the message of Jesus Christ to people in all walks of life.

Tom Shipp cared about alcoholics because he cared about all people. He did not see alcoholics as a separate race of condemned sinners but simply as human beings who had a problem which could be solved. He spent his life trying to help them. Before there were sufficient community organizations to care for alcoholics, he often brought them into his home. He listened and empathized with their problems in a way that was rare for a nonalcoholic to be able to do. He never gave up. He never stopped caring.

So it should not come as a surprise to learn that in the process of writing this book, Tom Shipp also went beyond the call of duty. He planned *The Trouble With Alcohol* even as he led his congregation of 8,000 to begin building a new sanctuary. He found time to work on it as he became a founding member of the Mayor's Public Inebriates Committee for the City of Dallas—a group which sought better solutions than jail for alcoholics arrested by the police.

During the year in which *The Trouble With Alcohol* was being completed, Tom Shipp suffered several bouts of ill health. But even when he was hospitalized, he continued to work on his book.

"I hope that *The Trouble With Alcohol* can serve as a bridge across the present gap between lay groups like Alcoholic Anonymous and the professionals who want to help," he often said. "I want to enable alcoholics, who are presently left to choose between experts or lay persons, to find the help they need from both groups."

The purpose of his book, he said, was to help alcoholics. He wished also to comfort those who come in contact with alcoholics and to inspire them to live in such a way that they might help both themselves and their loved ones. And he also hoped, with his writing, to encourage other ministers and professionals who work with alcoholics never to take alcohol away from troubled people until they give something to replace it—self-respect, the assurance of God's love, and faith in their fellow human beings.

In *The Trouble With Alcohol* the loving, generous, and hopeful spirit of Tom Shipp will continue to help those who are in trouble with alcohol, even though the author is now with his Saviour.